Praise for
Community College Success

"Isa Adney's new book addresses the questions and challenges she encountered on her journey as a community college student. They are the same questions countless community college students confront today as they navigate their own educational pathways. This is practical and down-to-earth counsel, not only for students, but for everyone who cares about student success."   –Eduardo J. Padrón
President of Miami Dade College

"Isa Adney speaks from experience in an authentic voice about her journey through the community college world, and has great advice for other community college students who want to connect and succeed in their own journeys. This book adds a useful and practical perspective to the current national conversation about student success and completion."   –Terry O'Banion, President Emeritus at the League for Innovation in the Community College

"Isa Adney writes with the authority of personal experience. She figured out how to turn the tears of her first, lonely days at her local community college – the only school she could afford – into the triumph of a top scholarship, a bachelor's degree and, soon, a master's. Community colleges exist to positively transform lives. This book will help students find out how." –Jay Hershenson, Senior Vice Chancellor
for University Relations and
Secretary of the Board of Trustees,
The City University of New York

"If you're ready to achieve more success in and out of school, then read and absorb the strategies in this important book. Isa is giving you strategies that can become a roadmap toward success, happiness and fulfillment. Brilliant information by a talented speaker, author and mentor!"   –James Malinchak
Featured on ABC's Hit TV Show, "Secret Millionaire."
Co-Author, *Chicken Soup for the College Soul.*
"Two-Time National College Speaker of the Year."
Founder, www.Malinchak.com

"*Community College Success* is an essential read for all community college students. Not only will this book guide readers to make the most of their college experience, it will inspire them to not settle for anything less then their dreams. Isa Adney's passion for empowering ALL students is contagious. She is truly a trailblazer in the world of education."
–Christine Hassler, Author of
20 Something, 20 Everything and *The 20 Something Manifesto*,
Life Coach, Professional Speaker

"Isa is passionate, committed, and driven to help students succeed in *Community College Success.* "
–Harlan Cohen, New York Times
Bestselling Author of *The Naked Roommate, and
107 Other Issues You Might Run Into In College*, and
*The Happiest Kid On Campus: A Parents Guide to
The Very Best College Experience (for you and your child)*

"Finally – a book tailor-made for first generation college students taking the first steps toward a productive and meaningful career. As members of a rapidly growing population, these students are in desperate need of a practical, friendly, and useful resource to guide them. Isa Adney's *Community College Success* fits the bill."
–Alexandra Levit, Author of
*They Don't Teach Corporate in College:
A Twenty-Something's Guide to the Business World*

"This is an important book for anyone who cares about working with students who are attending and completing community college credentials. Isa Adney provides a motivational story that is personal, yet relevant to many people: parents, students, higher education supporters, and educators."
–National Council on Student Development (NCSD)

"If Yoda were advising community college students, he'd repeat his advice to Luke Skywalker: 'Do or do not. There is no try.' In *Community College Success*, Isa Adney shows students how to set goals, get organized, overcome challenges, and create opportunities so they can "do" college well."
–Joanne Jacobs blogs at
Community College Spotlight (ccspotlight.org)

Additional Endorsements on page 171

Community College Success

You Are Not Alone

*How to Finish with
Friends, Scholarships, Internships,
and the Career of Your Dreams.*

Isa Adney

Printed in the United States of America
ISBN: 978-1-935254-62-1

Cover Photo: Ashley McCormick Photography
Cover Design: Dee Justesen
Book Design by Nadene Carter

First printing, 2012

Contents

INTRODUCTION
How Community College Changed My Life, and
How it Will Change Yours 1

ABOUT THE BOOK 8

SECTION I - PEERS 10

CHAPTER 1
Do You Want Fries with That?
Why Drive-Thru Education Isn't Enough 11

CHAPTER 2
The Awkward Five Minutes 19

CHAPTER 3
How Joining Clubs Can Help You Soar 27

CHAPTER 4
Why Everyone Should Want to be President 35

CHAPTER 5
Choosing a Major 41

CHAPTER 6
The New Kid Again 53

CHAPTER 7
The Alumni Advantage 61

SECTION II—PROFESSORS 66

CHAPTER 8
Translators of the College Language 67

CHAPTER 9
Getting to Know Your Professors–
The Mystery of Office Hours 73

CHAPTER 10
I Should Just Transfer to the
Closest University, Right? 81

CHAPTER 11
How Professors Helped me Win a $110,000 Scholarship
and How They Can Help You Do the Same 85

SECTION III—PROFESSIONALS 90

CHAPTER 12
Where Have You Come From, and
Where are You Going? 91

CHAPTER 13
The Best Way to Discover Your Perfect Career
(and Avoid a Miserable One) 97

CHAPTER 14
The Value of a Professional Mentor 103

CHAPTER 15
Okay, Hidden Job Market,
"Ready or Not Here I Come!" 109

CHAPTER 16
Who Should You Talk To, and
Where Do You Find Them? 111

Chapter 17
The Magic of Advice—How to Get Anyone to
Talk to You 117

CHAPTER 18
The Art of Setting an Appointment 127

CHAPTER 19
How to Talk to Strangers—Making the Most of
Your Informational Interview 131

CHAPTER 20
The End is Only the Beginning. 135

STUDENT STORIES 141

RECOMMENDED RESOURCES 157

ACKNOWLEDGEMENTS 165

ABOUT THE AUTHOR 169

Introduction

How Community College Changed my Life, and How it Will Change Yours

ON MY FIRST DAY of community college, I cried like a little girl. Like so many students I've met since then, I didn't want to be there. I felt alone, dejected, and lost. I also *ended* my community college experience with crying—on graduation when the president announced I'd won the $110,000 Jack Kent Cooke scholarship. Dozens of people surrounded me with hugs and tears. I had friends, money, and a future.

All this didn't happen to me through luck or because I'm a super-genius (see my SAT scores). The secret to success isn't good fortune or a high IQ—it's people. No matter how technological our world gets, the best opportunities in life will always happen through people. And the people you meet in community college will change your life.

Millions of dollars in scholarships, incredible opportunities, and jobs are available to students who know how to connect with others. You deserve to be one of those students. It's up to you to find the right people, ask for help, and admit you can't do it alone.

How do you find these people? How will you know what to say? How can you convince them to talk to you? And how does a conversation lead to hundreds of thousands of dollars and a life you can't even imagine? I'll show you.

But first—to know where you're going, it's important to know where you've come from. I want to share a little about me so you'll understand my background. As you read my story, I want you to consider your own story. Why are you in college? What barriers lie within your background? What opportunities? Only *you* have lived your life, and your personal story can teach you much about what holds you back, what pushes you forward, the things you value, and which problems in the world you want to fix.

I grew up in a lower-middle class family and attended a high school where only 25 percent of the students go to college. My socio-economic status and family history never entered my consciousness growing up, but the year my grandpa died changed everything for me.

After his death I learned more about how he and my grandma moved from Puerto Rico to New York before my father was born to make a better life for the Rosado family. My grandfather worked as a janitor for most of his life; my grandma was a maid. My dad made it into the open doors of community college, but never transferred to a university. He sacrificed and worked diligently as a case manager for a law firm, while my stay-at-home mom, my two younger brothers, and I lived on his income. Even though we were a lower-middle class family, I never felt disadvantaged. I remember once being around a rich girl and for a moment sensing she would have more opportunities in life than I could expect. That moment lasted for a millisecond while my mind came up with a satisfactory rationale—possibly the most naïve thought I've ever had in my life: *Even if people grow up in rich families, we will all start on the same level. We'll all be poor college kids and have to make it on our own … right?*

Wrong.

When I transitioned from my diverse community college to a small private school and began working for a tutoring center, for the first time I saw the advantages bestowed on people who grow up with money. Their college-educated parents pay for SAT tutoring, take them to college orientation, and guide them through the college process. Their parents have built-in professional connections for incredible internships and jobs.

These students receive professional guidance from parents who can teach them how to choose majors, get educated, and make money. They have free time in college to get involved, build relationships, and build resume experience. They know professionals and understand a wide variety of careers, which helps them choose a path in life. And in some cases (something I never understood), people who come from wealth pass down what they have through generations. When my grandma died, my family had a yard sale of her stuff to pay for the funeral. In wealthy families, when someone passes away the family receives money, stock, and other assets—giving them additional means to launch their own endeavors and enjoy financial security.

You might be thinking, *duh!* But I can honestly say that early in my college career I truly believed I had every opportunity to reach my goals, and that the playing field was fair and even. Obviously, I was wrong. Even though the playing field wasn't always fair, that didn't mean I still couldn't win.

But I didn't figure this out right away.

And that's why I ended up crying on the industrial carpet of my local community college. I felt so alone walking in there with my two-page application and a broken heart. This was not the idyllic college experience I imagined. I was supposed to be entering a lively freshman orientation, meeting new friends I'd have for life, picking out my classes and fresh books, and moving into the first place I could call my own. Instead, I was 15 minutes from home sitting in a small waiting room with strangers of all ages who looked as lost and alone as I felt. *How did I get here?*

I worked hard in high school and, overall, had a great experience. I joined the dance team, was a part of a small honors program, graduated fifth in my class, and was voted most likely to succeed. However, I knew nothing about the prestige and benefits of various universities, so when it came time to apply for colleges I naively applied to a small, idyllic, right-on-the-beach private school because my parents said I could go to college wherever I wanted. They said they would take out loans for my education because they believed in me. At the time, I was young and eager to take advantage of that offer.

You may be wondering why, if I came from a low-income family, my parents were able and willing to take out loans for wherever I wanted to attend college. The truth is, they were willing—but not necessarily able. However, that didn't stop them. I came from a family of sacrifice. And as a family that had been through hardship and gone into debt for many horrific things, they didn't blink an eye when it came to going into debt for something good.

When I was in high school, my younger brother, Tito, who was in seventh grade at the time, came home one day complaining of a stomach ache. The pain intensified, and when he began screaming and writhing in pain my mom rushed him to the hospital. They sent him home, saying he had food poisoning. The next morning he woke up paralyzed from the waist down from bacteria that migrated from his stomach to his spine.

A few months later my second youngest brother Robby, who was four years old at the time, had a seizure, shaking and foaming at the mouth, in my parents' bed at 4 a.m. My dad woke me up at 5 a.m., letting me know my mom had just left with my little brother in an ambulance, and for the first time I saw my father break. He cried and said, "I can't take this anymore."

That year drained my family mentally, emotionally, and financially. Tito was in the hospital for weeks and underwent months of physical therapy, including a grueling few months in a wheelchair that almost broke us all. Robby was diagnosed with epilepsy. The trauma of watching a small child have a seizure in your arms and having to give him four large pills every morning was rough on my parents. At the time I was too young to grasp the full gravity of what they endured. I had not yet known death, and my optimistic nature forced me to believe that no matter what, my brothers would be okay. And, thankfully, they were. Tito not only walked (something few in his condition would ever do) but also found a passion for skateboarding and now is the successful manager of a national skate and surf shop. Robby no longer has seizures and is in high school.

The years went by and with my parents' willingness to help further my education, I prepared to enter college. Three weeks before I would move into my new dorm, I was packed, excited, and ready to embark on this great adventure. On a bright summer morning, I sat at our white kitchen table opening the mail that arrived for me. I chose to open the crisp white envelope from my new college first. Inside was my freshmen schedule. I looked at the classes I would attend in a few weeks, and then read about the fun and lively orientation activities. But with the next page, a dark cloud descended. This was the bill for my first year of college. And I'll never forget what that number looked like, typed in small 12-point font, but so big to me.

$25,000.

In that instant, everything changed. I thought about Tito in a wheelchair; my parents sleeping on hospital couches; Robby shaking; and my dad crying in the hallway outside my bedroom saying, "I can't take this anymore." I thought about how they often sat at this very kitchen table struggling to decide which medical bills to pay and which ones they'd have to defer. And I asked myself: *Am I willing to add $100,000 to their debt for my education?* I knew the answer before I asked the question.

No.

So that was it. I unpacked my bags and drove to the local community college, searching for an affordable alternative. And I cried. Not because I regretted my decision, but because I didn't know what to do next or how to make the most of my choice.

More of my story is woven throughout these pages as I show you how I learned to take full advantage of my choice and finish college with friends, scholarships, internships, and the career of my dreams.

Community colleges have historically been an incredible gateway for access. Yet, sadly, those who don't understand, think they are schools where anyone can get in, thereby assuming they are colleges without prestige or high standards. That tide is changing as people begin to realize the crucial role community colleges (and state colleges) play in our national economy. More importantly, they play a role in helping incredible students rise above average and achieve a first-class education they might otherwise miss. Community colleges are filled with bright, intelligent students, professors who care and enjoy teaching, and staff who are in tune with the community and know how their college can improve lives.

After a year in community college, I began telling people it was like a private-school experience at public-school cost. As you will read, the small class sizes and personal attention I received were integral to my success. In this economy, saving such a substantial amount of money during those first two years of college can prevent loads of unwanted debt.

Community college is a smart choice. These schools don't let just anyone in … they accept *everyone* who wants an education. That's something to be proud of. The next step, however, is to make sure all those eager, worthy students are walking out with their goals met and a degree in hand. That's where I come in. I want to do more than help you finish—I want to help you finish with friends, scholarships, internships, and the career of your dreams. I want you to finish because you're excited and motivated about what your community college education will do for your future. Whether you leave with a two-year vocational degree, a bachelor's degree, or go all the way to your Ph.D., I want to make sure you do it with fire and passion, knowing you've found something worthy of your energy, sacrifice, and attention.

The pursuit of a college education is changing because so many students must work, support families, live off campus, and juggle their private lives while attending school. However, the energy and attention required for a college education hasn't changed—and thus we must all figure out how to balance our lives while taking full advantage of an education that has the potential to catapult us wherever we want our lives to go.

Where do you want to go? Do you know?

I will help you get there.

Are you thinking you don't have enough time to focus on college?

I will help you.

Do you know how you're going to pay for college?

I will help you.

Do you know how to interact in the professional world, land a job, and find a career that's right for you?

I will help you.

Inside this book you'll find the answers you need to make the most of your college experience, your talents, and most importantly, your life. These answers are unique. They aren't about studying harder, having a high IQ, or beating the system. The answers—the secrets—are about the people all around you, including the ones you don't know yet. Specifically—your peers, professors, and professionals. Any successful person can easily name ten people who helped him succeed. I can name twenty. We are social, interconnected beings who need one another. We have so much to learn from each other, and at no other time in life are so many people willing to help you.

Yet, sadly, not every student takes advantage of this hidden wealth. If you are like me and come from a low-income family, if you are the first in your family to attend college, or if you are a minority student, you need these people in your life more than you know. They will help you break barriers, make money, learn about careers you didn't know existed, get you into universities or careers you thought were beyond your reach, and show you how to succeed beyond your wildest dreams.

You only need one thing to shape your life into what you know it's meant to be: You must *want* to rise above average and make the most of your college experience and your future.

I cannot teach desire, passion, perseverance, or diligence, but if you have these qualities, I will help you succeed beyond your wildest dreams. I also know, if you're reading this right now, you are that person. You're the kind of college student who inspires me every day. You are why I do this. And I know you'll take what's in this book and do great things with your life. Thank you for making the extra effort to create your life and succeed in your education. I promise I won't let you down.

So, new friend, it's time to turn the pages and begin meeting people who will change your life.

About the Book

This book is organized in three sections, based on the category of people who will help you achieve success: peers, professors, and professionals. Some chapters could stand alone, and combine several categories, such as Chapter 5 on how to choose a major, and Chapter 7 on how to connect with alumni. However, the chapter placement is meant to help you keep in mind the most important point of this book—asking the right people for help. Peers, professors, and professionals can help you in almost every aspect of college and your future success, but each section emphasizes who will help you the most with a specific part of your life.

This book is for community college students, but the core concepts can help anyone who's looking for success at any stage of life. You can apply the tools and tips in this book for the rest of your life. You'll notice the section on transferring from community college comes relatively early in the book—Chapter 6 —because transferring isn't the end; it's another beginning.

Throughout the book you'll find special notes about links to
www.isaadney.com/freestuff
for exclusive resources just for my readers.

And finally, you'll find quotes from real community college students who agreed to share their stories, experiences, and advice. They are my friends who make up our online community at facebook.com/ccsuccess. I hope you'll join us. These students have won more than 72 prestigious awards, including the Jack Kent Cooke Undergraduate Transfer Scholarship, the Guistwhite Scholarship, and the ALL-USA Academic Team, and over $750,000 in scholarship funding. They all started out scared and wondered where their lives were going, but they eventually figured out how to invest in themselves and learn from the students around them. These students have great advice to share with you. At the end of the book you'll find more stories and advice from these incredible people, plus my favorite resources to help you in your journey toward success.

Section I—Peers

MICHELLE
"Making friends is an essential key for success in college."
—Quinnipiac University

Chapter 1

Do You Want Fries With That?
Why Drive-Thru Education Isn't Enough

ERICA

"Having friends and getting involved outside class were two of the most vital things that helped me in college. My peers helped me study, kept me accountable to attend class when I didn't feel like going, and opened up amazing opportunities for me."

—Seminole State College of Florida & Florida State University

GO TO CLASS. Go home. Go to Work. Repeat. Sound familiar? This is the typical routine for a commuter student—and this lifestyle is a recipe for failure and dropout. The truth is, students who do not fully engage in their college experience will never be able to compete with students who have that luxury. While every student has life circumstances that affect her ability to get involved and engaged in the college campus, every student can do *something* extra. Each student *must* do something extra. As Thomas Friedman said, "The age of average is over."

The curve is steadily rising, and as a result, "everyone needs to raise his or her game just to stay in place, let alone get ahead. What was an average performance in the past will not earn an average grade, an average wage, or a middle-class standard of living."[1] We are officially in "the age of 'extra'."

---

1   p.134 *That Used to Be Us* by Thomas L. Friedman and Michael Mandelbaum

This book is all about *extra,* so you must remember that average won't cut it. I have a saying: Do not get comfortable with average. You are more than average. Rise above average.

The average student just goes to class and returns home. You are more than average. The average student doesn't make it through college. You are more than average. The average student can't find a job after graduation. You are more than average. The average student doesn't bother making new friends. You are more than average.

Drive-thru education isn't enough, and the first step beyond average is connecting with your peers and making new friends. Why? Because the diversity, relationships, and connections you experience with your peers will give you support to manage your life when things get rough, as well as open your eyes to opportunities you never knew existed.

GRACE

"By making friends, I've been able to network and find out so much more about the college. My friends also gave me information for opportunities, such as the honors program and helped me get into the program. Friends make life at college so much more fun."
—Seminole State College of Florida

When I started community college I just attended class and went home. I didn't know there was anything more. Then a student came up to me after class and said, "Hey, we have a Phi Theta Kappa meeting after this class, and I think you'd make an amazing officer. Will you come?" I was flattered and thought *hey, why not?* That brief interaction after class led me to become president of Phi Theta Kappa and later win the $110,000 Jack Kent Cooke scholarship. Peers do make a difference.

So you need to make friends. Sounds simple, right? Community colleges are often filled with old high school friends and vibrant student life programs. However, though many community college students want to find new friends beyond the high school crowd, they aren't sure how to break out. Some stick to one or two pals and never feel the need to meet new people. Others hang out with friends who don't attend college and thus have no need to meet other people. Many feel isolated and alone and figure community college is just about going to class, nothing more. And of course, let's not forget the students who have so much going on in their lives that they make immense sacrifices to even attend classes, without any time for new friends. Which student are you?

I understand all the reasons for not making new friends and they're all incredibly valid. But if you close this book now, still asking, *"How is making friends going to help me succeed?"* you'll miss out. Because this isn't another college success book about how to study and get good grades. Those consequences will flow naturally from the strategies, secrets, and people nestled in these pages.

David

"Making friends in college helped me tackle math and made the college experience delightful. I found the more fun I had, the stronger my desire to succeed grew."
—College of the Sequoias in Visalia & University of California at Merced

Why do you need to make friends and connect with peers in college? Because the students who are lucky enough not to be working while in college are making friends and building networks that will enrich their college experience, help them develop and understand the perspectives of others, guide them toward new opportunities, help them get jobs in the future, and motivate them to stay in school. Sadly, at the time this book was written about 50 percent of community college students never finish their degree. While I'm sure a myriad of financial, academic, and life reasons lead to this depressing statistic, I know many of those students would stay and complete their degrees if only they felt connected; if only they had friends and a community to help when things got too hard; if only they had people to listen, believe in them, and tell them they can make it through that math class. If only they had friends to say, "We'll miss you too much if you leave." You can make that difference in someone's life, and others can make that difference for you. Ironically, I think sometimes the "community" is lacking in community colleges because everyone is so busy.

NAHIRIS

 "My family, friends and professors made a significant impact. They were always there to challenge and encourage me whenever I doubted myself."
—College of DuPage &
Boston University School of Medicine

Making friends comes naturally in high school because we spend eight hours a day with the same people. While many students are overjoyed to leave high school for college, don't worry if you find yourself missing that sense of high-school community and feel a secret loneliness—I did. Whether you're at a community college or a commuter at a university, when you live off campus it's difficult to create meaningful connections. Unlike kindergarten, where you easily bond on the swings or over shared love of a favorite color, meeting new friends in college presents a challenge.

Why bother with this extra stuff? Why not just go to class and go home and go to work?

Because that formula isn't working.

No matter how advanced technology becomes, we will always be a part of a world that thrives and advances through interpersonal connections. Who you know, how you relate, and how you communicate will affect your ability to succeed more than anything else. While some people have natural abilities or belong to a socio-economic class that makes this easier—I believe it can be learned. All you need is the motivation to succeed and the understanding that you can't do it alone. We need other people, and college is an incredible place to develop a network that will help you succeed in college and beyond. I will help you build that community.

Having friends in college is also fun; college should be fun, and I don't mean the kind of "fun" that leads to passed out college kids lying on the grass after partying all night. I mean the kind of fun that makes you feel your life matters, makes you enjoy what you're doing, and helps you feel purposeful. I'm referring to fun that causes you to feel confident and content in who you are, so that you know the hard stuff is worth it. Having friends brings the kind of fun that stems from vibrant conversations, an inside joke with a group, or a new idea that percolates after talking with a classmate. I will show you how to have that kind of fun.

Community college is a gift. Your classes are a gift. The new faces sitting around you on day one are also gifts. But they will stay wrapped up if you don't take the initiative to unpack them. *You* must take that initiative, because this book is all about you. Only you have lived your life. Only you have the skill, talent, and personality to make your contribution to the world.

MIKHAIL

> *"Making like-minded friends not only offers solace in times of trouble, it also keeps you focused on your goals, because your friends most likely have similar propensities toward success."*
> —Valencia College & The University of Tampa

Though the community college culture is often defined by the-go-to-class-go-home routine, you can change it. You can be the one to start a conversation. You can be the one who keeps another student from dropping out, or perhaps you'll meet someone who keeps you from dropping out. One pebble can make waves.

The rest of this book will show you how.

What Students are Saying

JOSHUA

"*Making friends in college helped me a lot. I do not think I would have made it through my Differential Equations class without them.*"

—Pensacola State College

GARY

"*Making friends and getting involved helped me be successful in college. It's nice to know others are going through the same things you are, and it's great to have people you can rely on.*"

—Jefferson College & University of Tampa

NAHIRIS

"*Making friends in college made all the difference. I surrounded myself with positive and passionate people who encouraged me to follow my dreams and challenge myself. They helped me improve my English and made going to school fun!*"

—College of DuPage &
Boston University School of Medicine

MELISSA

"*Without my friends, I wouldn't have made it through my classes or found out about Phi Theta Kappa and the opportunities it gave me. I know it's cliché that the people you befriend in college can become lifelong friends, but that's what I have now.*"

—Front Range Community College

JOSE

"*Making as many friends as possible gave me a remarkable support network both academically and socially.*"

—Essex County College &
Georgia Institute of Technology

HAINTSO

"*Making friends in college has helped me discover new resources I didn't know existed.*"

—Wayne State University

SUNIL

"Making friends is extremely important. Having a social life to help relieve the stress of a full schedule is vital. It's also important that the friends you make want to see you succeed and are not a hindrance."

—Broward College

Chapter 2

The Awkward Five Minutes

LINDA

"Making friends has kept me sane throughout college. Friends are the best support system during these years, because they understand what you're going through and often have great advice to help you overcome anything."
—Miami Dade College & Georgetown University

I'LL NEVER FORGET my first day at community college. The class was Western Civilization with about twenty students, and I sat in the second row. I remember thinking: *So this is college; I'm really here.* Silence filled the room. No one spoke. We all sat there, feeling new and awkward, waiting for the professor to show up. I desperately wished someone would say something—I so wished I had the courage to say something. And then, suddenly an obviously pregnant, dark-haired girl started a conversation with the girl next to her. She was so sassy and funny, and I remember feeling comforted. After she broke the ice, everyone else started talking, and with every class we became more than classmates—we became a learning community.

We all talked to each other every day before class—sometimes about the reading assignment, wondering if there would be a pop quiz, and sometimes about whatever was going on in the world or our lives. I began looking forward to that five minutes before the professor arrived.

Not all my classes were like this. In many, those awkward five minutes lasted through every class, all semester. In those classes no one spoke or took the time to get to know anyone else, because we all felt a little scared, lonely, and bored.

JEREMY

"Having such a high caliber of friends for the first time really helped me. I had never been friends with college students or grads before. They pushed me to succeed and continue school."
—Pikes Peak Community College & Colorado State University (Pueblo)

Often, I wished to be a more naturally outgoing person who could break the ice and bring a class community together. I didn't realize until later that I didn't need to be a super outgoing person to accomplish that. I could just be myself, and you can, too.

Once I figured this out, I began enjoying my college classes much more. I started conversations in every class. I made new friends. We shared stories, we shared our lives, and it was beautiful. I met a diverse group of people and learned perspectives I'd never encountered in my small world. The exposure to such variety made me a better person.

How many community college students drop a class because they think no one will notice? How many drop out of college because they feel disconnected? How many more students would do well in class if they had a study group? How many would participate in class if they felt part of a learning community? And how many more students would graduate if they knew they'd be graduating with their friends?

Friendship is a strong force in high school and four-year universities—so why should community college be any different? Yet, when you're a commuter it's easy to fall into the trap of seeing class as a utility—just a quick hour and fifteen minute chunk of the day when you drive, listen, maybe discuss a bit, and then drive home. No need to chat. No need to make friends. You'll be leaving in two years anyway, right? You need to get in and get out as fast as you can.

Bad idea.

JOSE

"Support from my family and friends, plus my academic determination, gave me the will to succeed, especially when my immigrant status at the time didn't allow me to use any of the scholarships I was awarded."

—Essex County College &
Georgia Institute of Technology

When you meet, connect, laugh, and enjoy people in your community college class, you'll feel connected and alive. Community colleges bring together people from all walks of life, and getting to know them will change you. For many of you, this is the first time away from your small high school world. Here's your big chance to expand your mind and explore the lives and experiences of others. Experiencing a variety of cultures, lifestyles, and perspectives will not only make you a more well-rounded and likable person, but will also shape our world into a better community. We need you to connect.

So how do you make friends? Should you just wait for someone else to speak up? Should you start every class blabbering about your own life?

I'm sure you've guessed the answer is no.

We can't wait for an institution to add a more welcoming orientation, a first-year experience course, or a service-learning initiative. We need to do this ourselves—and it starts with you. It's so much easier than you think. You can learn to start a conversation with a stranger and feel comfortable about it. The more you practice, the better you get. Embrace the fact that you're scared, and don't be tempted to compare yourself to others. You don't have to have a "life-of-the-party" personality to make new friends in class. You don't have to feel 100 percent confident to speak up. And while others may seem uninterested or more confident than you, they're probably feeling as nervous as you are. Think of expanding your social skills in the same way you approach a new class. Give yourself assignments, like talking to one new person every day, and keep trying until you get it right.

Instead of focusing on yourself, move your focus to the people around you. The easiest way to make connections in your classes is to ask questions. You can address the whole group on the first day by asking questions such as:

Has anyone heard anything about this professor?

Has anyone heard anything about this class?

As time passes, you can ask the whole class about the homework—if anyone knows the answer to a certain question, or if anyone would like to join a study group for the upcoming test. Bonding over the commonalities you all share in a particular class is one of the easiest ways to connect. When you know when your first exam will be, take the initiative and ask the class either in person or via a group e-mail if anyone would like to study for the exam with you. Then, go to the library and find out how to book a private study room. Tell your classmates where and when you've reserved the study room and invite them to meet with you to study and practice for the upcoming exam. Remember, you'll always want to study on your own first. The study group is a chance to recall what you've studied, help each other with concepts you might have missed, and enjoy each other's company. And once the exam is finished, don't be afraid to invite everyone in the study group out to coffee or lunch to celebrate. Never underestimate the power of food to bring people together.

Group projects are also a fantastic way to connect with your classmates. Whenever you're in a group, go above and beyond to organize your gatherings and make an effort to meet in person. When you get together to work on your project, make an effort to get to know your group members. Make sure your project is done to the highest quality, but also use the time to connect. Schedule group meetings at local cafes or restaurants, have lunch together, or organize a group hangout to celebrate once the project is finished. Each class will usually have a project or experience that gives you something to talk about instantly with your classmates. Take advantage of every opportunity.

HAINTSO

> *"Making friends in college has helped me discover new resources I didn't know existed."*
>
> —Wayne State University

When you're talking to classmates in a group or to the entire class, other great conversation starters include upcoming local or campus events, holidays, sports, food, and music. You'll be amazed by how many people will respond to your questions, your study groups, and your invitations to join a conversation about a topic. Most students are desperate to connect and will be thankful someone had the courage to speak up. You'll be surprised by how many people's lives you can change by making them a part of a conversation.

If you're an introvert and the idea of asking questions to the entire class makes your heart skip a beat, start by conversing with the person beside you. Ask her why she chose this class, what her major is, when she'll graduate, and what she thinks of the class so far. Compliment her on something. Keep asking questions and find commonalities between the two of you. Listen to other people's stories and share yours. Be vulnerable and open up. Nothing encourages people to share their authentic selves more than hearing someone else share her own story. Be yourself and you give others the permission to do the same. [2]

Also, don't be afraid to casually listen to conversations around you. If two people are talking about a topic you're interested in, see if you can join the conversation. You obviously don't want to

---

2   This is a paraphrase from one of my favorite quotes by Marianne Williamson who says: "And as we let our own light shine, we unconsciously give other people permission to do the same."

interrupt in a rude way or seem creepy, and you'd never want to chime in if someone is having a deeply personal conversation. However, most people understand that conversations they have in a classroom will be heard, so they expect others to join in. The best way to do this is to wait for a pause in the conversation after someone says something you agree with. You can then turn around and say something like, "Sorry, I don't mean to butt in, but I just heard what you were saying and I totally agree," and then comment on why you agree by giving an example or a brief anecdote. This will usually endear you to the pair, and if they smile or comment on what you just said, you'll know you are welcome to join the conversation.

You never know what kinds of personalities you'll have in a classroom, and it's inevitable that not everyone will seem as friendly. While we should always have respect for everyone, we won't always want to be best friends with everyone. This is okay. Don't worry if someone brushes you off, doesn't join your study group, or is unresponsive to your questions. Just move on to another person and know it has nothing to do with you. We all connect in different ways and must reach out to a lot of different people to find the ones with whom we truly click. The more you have the courage to speak up and get to know people, the more you'll expand your social circle and discover amazing new relationships. You'll grow and mature as you give yourself a chance to deeply connect with new friends.

And finally, if you want to make friends, you need to look approachable—and part of that is turning off your cell phone. Not just when the professor starts talking, but *before you walk in.* I know this device offers comfort and gives you something to do while you're waiting for class to start; you can stay busy checking Facebook instead of feeling the awkward vibes of silence. Resist that temptation. Bask in the awkwardness and let it give you the courage to speak. Being on your phone sends a message that you don't want to be bothered—that you have no interest or desire to meet anyone. This is the message you send, even if it doesn't reflect who you are. Most of us unconsciously use our phones as shields against uncomfortable situations. Break this habit and you'll turn uncomfortable situations into incredible opportunities.

Technology offers many ways to connect, but it will never take the place of genuine conversation. Put your phone away and start looking people in the eye. See what you observe when you don't have that screen in front of your face. You may see loneliness behind those texting thumbs, and you may be the exact person someone else needs to talk to that day.

Crush your fear, turn off your phones, start study groups, invite people to things, speak up, and ask questions. We need to bring the community back to community colleges—and only you can do it. If you don't, no one else will. And if you become the hero—the defender of those awkward five minutes—you will also feel fulfilled and connected. You'll graduate and have friends to take pictures with and laugh with and connect with long after your community college experience ends. You'll have an experience to remember for the rest of your life. And not only will you change your life—you'll change someone else's.

What Students are Saying

SAMMIE

"In community college I was a shy student who didn't make friends easily, but I kept trying, and a group of amazing people asked me to join their study group. From that moment on, I had a support team."
—Indiana Vocational Technical College

VANESSA

"Making friends in college has helped me tremendously because they've been a support system. Friends help you build confidence and discover your unique self. That helped me a lot because I thought I was just average."
—Seminole State College of Florida & University of Central Florida

Chapter 3

How Joining Clubs Can Help You Soar

ANGELICA

> *"My biggest fear was getting involved and moving out of my comfort zone. Eventually I took the plunge and started attending club meetings and developing an open mind about meeting a new group of people. I also discovered leadership potential in myself I didn't know I had."*
> —Seminole State College of Florida &
> Stetson University

WHILE GROWING UP, I didn't have many opportunities to travel. We lived in Florida, so every vacation consisted of a forty-five-minute drive to the beach. Flying on an airplane seemed like a luxury for the rich and famous. This was something I desperately wanted to do, but I had no idea when I'd be able to afford a ticket. And then I had a chance to fly for free.

As President of the Pi Lambda chapter of Phi Theta Kappa, I was given the opportunity to fly to Nashville, Tennessee for the international convention. While this may not seem like a big deal to some people, it was a huge event for me. I'll never forget that first ascent into the clouds. For the first time in my life, I knew I was going places.

Had I not followed a classmate I barely knew to a Phi Theta Kappa chapter meeting, I would have missed that adventure.

However, joining a club on campus is about much more than free travel and making friends. Clubs are where opportunities happen. Whether it's an amazing trip, a scholarship, a job opportunity, or a great connection, you'll be amazed at how clubs can affect your life, but you'll never know if you just attend classes and go home. You'll never find out if you don't show up.

ALEX — no

AUSTYN

> *"I actually started the first psychology club on the UCF Sanford/Lake Mary campus. I also joined several clubs where I met lots of people. Being a part of clubs made me want to go to school more and led to higher grades."*
> —Seminole State College of Florida & University of Central Florida

At one of my first Phi Theta Kappa meetings I heard about the Jack Kent Cooke scholarship, and at those same meetings I met close friends who cried for me when I won the scholarship. Phi Theta Kappa helped me win dozens of awards and scholarships and helped me realize potential I never knew I had.

Joining a club will build your confidence, expand your college resume, and provide you with unforgettable experiences. Yet it's shocking how few students take advantage of these opportunities. Be the student who does.

ALEX

> *"The main reason I've been able to succeed in college is because I have friends with similar goals. Their motivation to succeed inspired me to work harder and accomplish my goals. Since they had similar goals they always could identify with my motives to succeed."*
> —Seminole State College of Florida & University of Central Florida

How do you start? It's so simple.

Go to your college's website and search for the student activities or campus life section, where you'll find a list of all the clubs on campus. Read through them and list the top five groups you find interesting:

Club Name	Meeting Day/Time	Contact
1.		
2.		
3.		
4.		
5.		

If you need more information, email or call the contact person listed on the website, or just show up to the next meeting or club event. During the next two weeks, make time to attend meetings that interest you and find a group that best suits you. Any club you find interesting will be helpful, but I highly recommend groups that involve your intended field, along with honor societies. I especially urge you to join Phi Theta Kappa. If you don't have the grades yet—aspire to them and make it happen.

NAHIRIS

"The best thing I ever did was join Phi Theta Kappa and become an officer in the chapter. From there, all doors were open for my success in community college and beyond."
—College of DuPage &
Boston University School of Medicine

If you can't locate the club listings on your college's website, find out where your college's student activities office is located and pay a visit. I recommend you do this anyway. The student activities staff members are there to help you find ways to supplement your college education and lead you toward success. And trust me—there's nothing we love more than a student who walks through our door saying she wants to get involved but doesn't know how.

Schedule an appointment with your student activities staff right now and let them guide you toward the best opportunities on your campus. You can make that appointment in person, by phone, or via email.

Now all you have to do is show up.

What Students are Saying

ASHLEY

"Getting involved changes how you view your school, from being a place you only attend classes into a place where you actually want to be."

—Pasco-Hernando Community College

JESSICA

"Joining clubs changes the way you see your college. I loved going to school every day knowing I was going to a club meeting."

—Seminole State College of Florida

CHRISTOPHER

"Networking and getting involved with a variety of organizations and people has expanded my outlook on life, developed my leadership and motivational skills, and developed me into the person I am today. My friends and colleagues are my support system."

—Rochester Institute of Technology

MELISSA

"Having grown up in the military, I always had a hard time keeping up with my friends as we moved all over the world. But I know now, that as a part of the Phi Theta Kappa family, I automatically have friends wherever I go, and they understand me and my quirks."

—Front Range Community College

ANGELICA

"Being able to afford college was one of my biggest obstacles. I was able to get scholarships by getting involved and serving the community. Giving back to the community is rewarding on many levels and scholarships just happen to be one of them."
—Seminole State College of Florida &
Stetson University

ASHLEY

"I was scared to get involved. Now I'm amazed at all the new doors that being involved actually opens for me."
—Pasco-Hernando Community College

SHIENA MARIE

"I've won numerous awards for academic excellence, leadership, and community service. My advice? Be involved. Get your face and name out in the community. There are a lot of people out there just waiting to give you an award. Trust me."
—Northwest Florida State College

SUNIL

"I joined SGA after making the decision to be fully engaged in school and all it has to offer. At that point I had to quit my job and force myself to use clubs and scholarships to supplement the income. It was a risky move, but it paid off!"
—Broward College

SANA

"I truly didn't want to attend community college because I didn't believe I would get the full college experience; however, I was proven wrong when I got involved with student activities."
—Seminole State College of Florida

KRISTINA

"I joined many clubs and it actually helped me become more outgoing."
—Seminole State College of Florida

STEVE

"*It's important to make friends in college who have similar ambitions to your own. Befriending other focused, driven, serious students helps you maintain your values. Friends of this sort also become an incredible resource for editing your papers, helping with your transfer applications (if you are a two-year college student), and providing feedback for school projects and extracurricular activities. Not to mention the added benefit of having people with which to unwind after stressful periods like finals, who won't distract you from being successful.*

"*I was fortunate enough to make such friends, and it benefited me immensely. The friends I made in community college continue to motivate my success now that I've moved on.*"

—Valencia College & Emory University

MICHELLE

"*I was the Officer of Service for the Phi Theta Kappa National Honor Society. Being part of a group of high achievers helped me as an older person. Keeping a high GPA furthered my goals with more successes than I ever imagined.*"

—Quinnipiac University

PAUL

"*As my Dad was not in the picture growing up, I didn't have the guidance I needed on how to survive the college system. The support I gained through Phi Theta Kappa Honor Society gave me the encouragement, guidance, and accountability I needed.*"

—Columbus State Community College

HEATHER

"*The most important thing besides your studies is to get connected. Connect with people whose goals are similar to yours and create a support system for yourself. Being part of organizations like Phi Theta Kappa can give you the support you need.*"

—Mesa Community College &
Northern Arizona University

JOHN

"My friends in college encouraged me to apply for scholarships and get involved with leadership and volunteer service programs. Because of them, my confidence level grew. They always pushed me!"

—Seminole State College of Florida &
University of Central Florida

VANESSA

"I was involved with many clubs. They all helped me spread my wings and be open-minded to everything in life. I learned what it takes to be a leader and how to work with a team. You also get really close to people who become your best friends."

—Seminole State College of Florida &
University of Central Florida

GRACE

"Joining and becoming an officer for Phi Beta Lambda (Future Business Leaders of America) was one of the best decisions I've made since I started community college. Being a secretary for PBL opened so many doors. I've met so many new people and it helped me figure out what I want to do with my life. It has also given me new confidence in myself."

—Seminole State College of Florida

ALEJANDRA

"Becoming president of the Nursing Students Association at the University of Miami helped me get a nursing internship at a local hospital."

—Palm Beach State College &
University of Miami

Chapter 4

Why Everyone Should Want to be President

HEATHER

"Being president of Phi Theta Kappa not only boosted my confidence, it gave me the courage to take on the world!"

—Mesa Community College & Northern Arizona University

ONCE YOU BEGIN attending meetings for the clubs of your choice, resist the temptation to just sit in the back of the room and watch. It's okay to quietly observe during your first meeting or two if that makes you feel more comfortable, but as soon as possible you should become more active by meeting the officers and asking how you can be involved. For example, you might share fund-raising ideas, organize a community service project, help with an event, lead a committee, or assist with paperwork. Try out a few activities with the club and see how they fit. As you get comfortable and engage with the group, it's then time to think about taking on a leadership role as an officer and working your way up to president. At many community colleges you can begin in an officer role right away and then run for president the following semester. The key is to engage with the club first, but also move quickly in finding leadership roles, because two years at a community college goes by quickly.

One advantage of community colleges is the fact that many students are too busy to stand out by becoming president of a club or starting their own group. Community college students have access to state, national, and international leadership positions they rarely know about. You'll soon learn why attaining such leadership positions is vital to your success, as these positions have the potential to win you thousands of dollars in scholarship money and full-ride acceptance to the most prestigious four-year colleges and universities. Four-year colleges want top leaders and will pay to have you. And becoming one of these leaders is easier than you think. It only requires a bit of courage.

LINDSEY

"I was shy. Starting community college at the age of 21 was awkward because most students were younger. After learning about Phi Theta Kappa from an older student, I joined.

"The next semester I became secretary and had an amazing experience. The semester after, I was elected president and am president again for the second consecutive semester.

"I was scared to put myself out there with PTK, but after realizing the benefits that came with it. I felt no hesitation. I researched every aspect and threw myself into doing everything I could with PTK and my classes."

—St. Johns River State College

Showing up to a club or campus event truly is half the battle. The other half—the part that will help you reach your dreams, get paid to go to college, and open doors to opportunities you don't even know exist right now—is to run a club. Most students are content to attend club meetings without taking on responsibilities. That's why clubs are happy to find people who want to be leaders.

Yes, you can be president of a club. Students who take on these leadership roles are the ones who are most successful in community college and beyond. Read the biographies of students who win scholarships. You may already know they are campus leaders. However, you may not realize that such a leader is inside you.

Even if you've never joined a club in your entire life, you can lead one. No particular type of student is good at leading a group. No special amount of prior experience is needed to be a successful club president. All you need is desire and willingness to make the club successful. If you care enough about the club's mission, you needn't have any idea what you're doing.

When I decided to become president of our campus Phi Theta Kappa chapter, I was scared and uncertain I could actually do the job. I was truly clueless. I jumped into a small officer position and learned along the way. After being in Phi Theta Kappa for one semester, I wasn't sure if I was ready to be a chapter president, but I also realized this was my last chance, because I'd be graduating before the next election. And the same thing that gave me the courage to take an officer position gave me incentive to run for president: encouragement from my friends. I knew I'd be able to ask for help and I wouldn't be doing anything on my own—I would be part of a team. My decision to run for president turned out to be one of the best choices I ever made.

HEATHER

"Being the V.P of Finance, the V.P. of Scholarship, and then President of Phi Theta Kappa Omicron Beta Chapter brought new, exciting adventures and opened doors for me that I never thought I'd have at forty years old."
—Mesa Community College & Northern Arizona University

Leading a club doesn't take that much work, especially if you learn to delegate. You'll have a team and an advisor to help you achieve the club's goals, and you'll probably find that being deeply involved increases your motivation and involvement in the entire college experience. You'll make valuable connections, build deeper relationships, spend more time on campus, and feel motivated about going to class and getting good grades. People will count on you, which feels good. And the best part? You'll find something you're good at and develop skills and friendships that will serve you for the rest of your life.

MELISSA

"I joined Phi Theta Kappa and soon became the Public Relations Officer. I am now the president of my chapter. Because of this, I've developed new leadership skills, become an expert at multi-tasking, and found wonderful friendships at my college and throughout the world."
—Front Range Community College

Are you ready to be a president? You're probably still scared, right? It's okay. Everyone is. But the successful students are the ones who jump into the college experience, despite feeling inadequate. If you wait for those feelings to go away, you'll be waiting forever.

Now is the time for you to jump in. And you're not alone, because I'm here to help. The steps to being a club president are simple:

1.   Follow the suggestions in Chapter 3 (e.g., check out five clubs and meet with a student activities staff member).
2.   Tell the student activities staff member which club(s) you find interesting and ask for advice on what you need to do to become president of one of those clubs.
3.   Choose the club that interests you most. If it doesn't exist, talk to your student activities staff member about starting your own. This is easier than you think and looks impressive on a college resume. You just need to be sure you're passionate about your club's mission so you can rally others around you to begin the adventure.
4.   Once you've attended a few club meetings and helped out at an event, introduce yourself to the current

president of the club and find out about the process to interview for, or run for, a club officer position.

5. Once you're in a club officer position, let the current president know you'd like to be president of the club next term. Ask his or her advice. Help the officers achieve club goals and support them as much as possible. Bring your unique personality to your current officer position and go above and beyond.

6. Attend leadership retreats or conferences to learn more about leadership and hone your skills.

ERICA

"My advisors and executive team gave me the confidence and courage to be student government president. They always showed me appreciation and never let me think for one moment there was anything in this world I couldn't do. They are the ones who gave me the strength and power to be a good leader."

—Seminole State College of Florida & Florida State University

If you haven't figured it out yet, the key to this entire book is learning how to ask for help. Success never happens alone, and people are so willing to help you. But sadly, too many students walk silently down the halls and never ask. Break that cycle. Start with your peers and your student activities staff. As I said earlier—there's nothing they love more than a student who walks into their office and says "I want to get involved in some groups, but I don't know how." You'll be a star in their eyes and they'll bend over backward to help you achieve your goals.

You *can* be a president. Your campus needs you, and you need your campus. Your two years of college will fly past, so be sure to start now.

Write it Into Existence

I want to be the president of _____

I will be president by_____

What Students are Saying

ANEAL

"Being president of the Student Government Association gave me a sense of purpose and the opportunity to meet people from different walks of life who taught me so much."

—Palm Beach State College

GARY

"As President of Phi Theta Kappa, many tasks require you to develop leadership skills. When I was younger I had a serious stutter, but I pushed myself through it and gained the confidence needed to run an organization like this."

—Jefferson College &
University of Tampa

SUNIL

"Being the president of the Student Government Association helped me gain courage and confidence."

—Broward College

ALEJANDRA

"I have been the president of three clubs. The first time I decided to run for presidency, I was very nervous. However, after being in charge of an organization and developing leadership skills, I became more confident. This confidence allowed me to run for the presidency in other clubs, and therefore enhanced my leadership skills even more through experience and mentoring from my club advisors."

—Palm Beach State College &
University of Miami

Chapter 5

Choosing a Major

SHIENA MARIE

"I feared I wasn't making the right choice in my major, and that I was just selecting something to please my parents. I had to realize I need to choose what makes me happy — this is my life to live and it's my decision to find my niche in life."
—Northwest Florida State College

YOU MAY BE WONDERING why I placed a chapter on choosing a major in the heart of the peer-to-peer connection section of this book. The chapter is here for two reasons:

1) When I was student activities coordinator at a community college, in addition to helping students get involved and encouraging them to become presidents of clubs, another topic constantly came up: Students struggled over choosing a major and why they wanted a college education in the first place. I wrestled with the same problems during my college years.

2) During my journey to find the major that worked best for me, I learned that recent graduates and fellow students in their senior year of college could be a tremendous resource.

Talking with professionals will certainly help you figure out your major. However, connecting first with your college peers can be the most enlightening step. Your fellow students are in the middle of experiencing their major *now,* including jobs, internships, and other opportunities. This should be part of your peer-to-peer connection.

In addition, this chapter had to come early. To transfer into the right program and connect with professors and professionals, you need a clear direction for your studies. The first step in finding that direction is to do your research and select a major as soon as possible.

Why You Must Choose a Major ASAP

College goes by quickly, and with increasingly tight financial aid regulations and career pathways, getting on the right track early can save you time and money. It may even save your future. The more you focus on a specific major and career, the more likely you are to finish college. You'll have a good reason to get up in the morning. You'll have a reason to break through barriers that stand in your way. You'll have a reason to study, and you'll know every class is moving you toward the goal of doing something with your life and finding an interesting career that contributes to the world. Wouldn't it be great to love attending college every day?

The Wrong Major — the Wrong Context Clues

If you're like most students, you chose your first major based on personal experience, things people have told you, and context clues within the major's name. For example, students often tell me something like, "I'm going to major in international business because I like to travel."

I then ask, "Are you interested in international economics, how to sell in a global economy, and classes in multinational business finance?"

"Um ... well ... not really," is the usual answer.

That's okay. I majored in "communications" because I liked people and liked to "communicate." If you're like me and come from a lower socio-economic class, you probably haven't been exposed to many careers or college majors. So you do the best you can, read the context clues, and try to select a major that seems to suit your interests. I completely understand how this happens. However, when it comes to choosing a college major, using context clues alone may lead you down a path with twists and turns you aren't prepared for.

Choosing a clear, defined academic and career pathway you're excited about is one of the most important ingredients to your personal success. But the perfect major and career are not out there waiting for you. You need to create what you want. This is similar to the theory of finding "the one." You can't sit around waiting for your perfect soul mate to come knocking on your door (unless you end up marrying the pizza guy ... but that's another story); you have to get out there, try different things, and meet new people. When it comes to choosing a major, keep in mind that jobs, careers, and college degrees are constantly evolving in our fast-paced world. You have to evolve with them.

So how do you choose? Should you pick the career you think will bring the most money? Should you choose what your parents want for you? What about the major that seems easiest or has the most convenient class schedule?

None of the above.

The most important factor, and the key to motivation and success, is to choose a major in which you have genuine interest and talent. To discover your interests and talents, you must ask for help, read, research, experiment, and, eventually—choose.

CHRISTOPHER

"I was scared entering college without having a major defined (I was undecided). After exploring and going through a special program for undecided students, I found my niche."
—Rochester Institute of Technology

Making the Choice

The first and best step when making your choice is to visit your college's career center to meet with a career counselor and take any personality and career tests they offer. While these tests aren't prescriptive, they will give you a great starting point. By using data from the tests for guidance, you can decide who to talk with, what to research, and which classes to experiment with.

The next step is to sign up as soon as possible for introductory electives that interest you. Like all of us, you'll struggle with some classes while others seem effortless and even fun. Notice your natural strengths and interests in classes and extra-curricular activities. What do people compliment you on the most? Where do you shine? When do you feel most alive? Chase those feelings and those fields of study.

For example, I always knew I loved writing and under-standing how people communicate, so a communications major was perfect for me. I loved almost every class in this field, and it led to winning awards, scholarships, and accolades because I chose something for which I had both interest and talent. I was able to shine. You will shine too if you figure out how to combine your interests and talents. Choosing a major because someone else says it's a good, stable, and profitable choice doesn't work. For example, although I knew the business major was projected to be more profitable, I also knew I had little interest or talent in investing, finance, and business plans.

Unfortunately, I've seen many students choose a major because someone else is pushing them down a certain path. I also find students choosing a major that the latest study reveals will guarantee a good salary. There's nothing wrong with wanting to make money and have a secure future, but I find too many students are terrified to repeat their parents' cycle of poverty. They choose a major to make a lot of money, only to find they aren't interested in that subject and end up failing classes and repeating the cycle they were so afraid of.

The best way to ensure a bright future is to choose a major based on who you are and where you want to go.

Keep in mind that even if you choose a major today, you may change your mind down the road, and once you have a job, you may switch careers a few times. That's okay. These changes mean you're still learning and willing to adjust. It doesn't mean you shouldn't choose now, because wandering aimlessly is almost a surefire path to the drop-out lane. Even if you do alter your major and career as you progress in your life, it's better to make slight adjustments to your goals as you learn more about yourself and the world, rather than jumping to extremes.

Researching Your Choice

To make the best initial choice, begin researching your prospective major(s) and connecting with junior and senior students, as well as recent graduates. Your goal is to see if the major fits with what you've learned about yourself so far. Before you reach out to peers in the majors that interest you, conduct the following online research:

1. Go to an online job board and type in the name of the major you're considering. See what positions come up and read the job descriptions. Ask yourself—"Would I want that job?"

2. Go to the website of the four-year college or university to which you plan on transferring and find their online college catalog.[3] Search for the section listing your major and the course descriptions. Read the course name and description of every required class and ask yourself: "If this was a title of a book or online article, would I want to read it in my free time?" If the answer is yes for at least 2/3 of the classes, you'll know you're on the right track. If not—keep exploring the online catalog and course descriptions.

Connecting with Peers in Your Major

Once you've chosen a prospective major (or two), it's time to seek out students at the universities you're considering for transfer and ask them questions like:

---

3   Most college catalogs are searchable online. The catalog lists all programs and majors, required courses, and the requirements for completion. The catalogs also provide important dates to help you stay on track. You should know the catalog of your community college and your intended transfer institution very, very well.

1. What do you like most about this major?
2. What do you like most about your college?
3. What is most challenging about this major?
4. Who are your favorite professors and why?
5. What kinds of personalities seem to do best in this major?
6. What kinds of internships have you or others gotten in this major?
7. What kinds of jobs do you think you'll be able to get after you graduate?

You might think—yeah those are good questions, but how will I find someone to ask? This is easier than you think, and you have many options:

1. Arrange a campus tour/class visit.
Contact the admissions department at the university and see if you can arrange a meeting, a campus tour, and/or visit a class. Keep emailing and contacting people until you get a response, and be sure to use the Internet. A bit of resourcefulness and creative searching will help you find who these people are and how to get in touch with them. Once you contact people at the college, let them know you'd like to talk to a student and ask a few questions about the major/program. If you're able to visit a class, turn to anyone who seems nice and ask if she will answer a few questions for you. I know this may sound intimidating, but you'll be surprised how many people will be delighted to talk to you. Think about it—if someone came up to you right now and asked your advice about how your college experience has been so far, how would you feel? Probably flattered that someone values your experience and opinion. This is how you will make others feel, and they'll be happy to help you.

2. Search an alumni database.
Ask your college if they have an alumni database, listing programs their graduates majored in or the colleges to which

they transferred. My university has this infomation. That's how I found many of my career mentors. If your college doesn't have such a database, ask about creating one, because community college students need to connect with alumni at transfer universities. Also, see if any of the clubs or organizations you're part of keep an alumni database listing students' majors and their contact information.

3. Social media.

Social media and the Internet are incredible resources for finding people. Try posting a status update on Facebook letting friends know you're trying to find someone who majored in XYZ. You can also connect with the university's Facebook page and ask if anyone who majored in XYZ would be willing to answer a few questions via email. Also, search for the major and university in the keywords section of LinkedIn.

LinkedIn.com is a key resource I used during my career search. This forum is essentially a Facebook for professionals, listing people's job history, resume information, and educational histories. We'll talk more about it in section three, but for now, go ahead and create a profile if you haven't already. Use a professional picture and information from your resume. (Hint: if you need help with the resume, make an appointment with your career counselor at your college.)

For your major search, browse LinkedIn profiles by entering your major in the keyword section of the advanced search and notice the careers of people who majored in that field. Note the companies they've worked for, internships they received, jobs they obtained right out of college, and what their job descriptions entail. Does anything grab you?

If you come across a profile that interests you, send that person a request to connect.[4] Do not use the standard request

---

4   LinkedIn prefers that you do not ask to connect with people you don't know, and you should abide by their rules and policies. They may ban you from connecting with others if you ask to connect with too many people who reject your request as this can seem spammy.

message, as it shows little effort. Instead, try a brief but genuine request, such as:

"Hi [insert name here], I see you majored in [insert major here] in college. I'm considering that major right now and I admire your career path. I'd love to learn from you and connect. Thanks so much. Sincerely, [insert your name here]."

Almost every request I've made like this has been accepted, and those people have become important friends.

If you don't want to connect on LinkedIn, you can often find a person's contact information by searching for his name on the staff directory on the company website where he works—or just Google the name. Be creative and fearless. You'll be surprised how many people will gladly respond—especially current students and young professionals, because they remember all too well how confusing it can be to choose a major.

Once someone in your prospective major accepts your request for advice, you can either arrange a 15-minute meeting or phone call, or send them the above questions via email. Let your new contacts know how much you appreciate their time and advice and make it all about them, not you. You'll gain much more if you let them do the talking. Whenever possible, make contact in person or on the phone. This gives you a more genuine connection and many long-term benefits. However, email can work as long as you do it right and don't use it as your default. Step outside your comfort zone and meet people.

I know all this connecting sounds like extra work, but I promise—the more you reach out to people when making decisions in your life, the more you'll understand why this is so important. Try it once and you'll see exactly what I'm talking about. Connecting with others who've done what you're about to do will enlighten you, teach you, and give you insider advice you couldn't get any other way.

When you hear from someone in a particular major, you'll know whether or not it's a good fit for you. You'll also hear about current industry trends and how the job market looks for the near future. You may even get a great internship lead, or an offer of help once you graduate. This is one of the best parts about connecting with someone in your major. You'll already have a friend at the university or in the business world—someone to show you around, help you connect with resources, and make a new and overwhelming experience more manageable. Also, knowing a successful person in the field you've chosen gives you a target to aim for. When you drag yourself out of bed for that 7 a.m. math class, you can say, "I've gotta do this if I want to be like her."

Whether you know without a doubt what you'll major in, or you feel more lost than ever, talking to people who've gone before will help you understand what you want.

Final Steps to Choosing Your Major

After you've done the above, I predict you'll be bubbling with excitement about the possibilities for your life. Now it's time to take action and take the final steps toward making your choice a reality. You need to contact two more people:

1. Meet the program director.

Arrange a meeting with the director of the program you're considering at the four-year college where you plan to transfer.[5] To find this person, search for the department head's email on the university website or ask an admissions counselor at the university to help arrange the meeting. If you don't live nearby, try to arrange a phone call. If that fails, you can use email.

When you meet the program director, you'll want to ask a few questions, similar to the things you asked your peers:

1. What is most challenging about this major?
2. What kinds of skills and personalities are most successful in this major?
3. What kinds of internships have past students received?
4. What kinds of jobs have past students found?

---

5   If you're planning to just get a two-year degree, meet with the program director at your community college.

Some of these program directors may be difficult to reach, but be persistent, and be brief. You may find the answers to some of your questions on the college website, or get the info you need from a knowledgeable admissions recruiter. The key is to get your questions answered and notice if the answers fit your interests and talents.

2. Meet with your community college counselor/advisor.
Once you've conducted research and feel confident in your major choice, you'll want to ensure you're on the right track to completing that major on time, with the credentials you'll need to transfer.

Go back to the university online catalog and print the academic plan that lists all the requirements for your major. Make an appointment with a community college counselor/ advisor and bring the academic plan with you to compare it with your current community college educational plan. Be sure you're on the right track to graduate from your community college and transfer seamlessly to your prospective four-year institution.

This will save you more time and money than you can imagine. Students who don't do this often take an average of six years to get their bachelor's degree. You don't want to be stuck taking extra classes after two years, or waiting an extra semester for a class to become available. Do not let this happen to you.

Knowing Your Major + Knowing Yourself = Motivation
Once you've done the research and chosen a major that fits your personality and talents, your motivation will ignite. Motivation is crucial in college, and without it you'll be hard put to complete your degree. It's paramount to have greater interests, greater purpose, and greater personal investment in your overall goal. Without this involvement you'll be challenged to get up in the morning and find purpose in each class, assignment, and exam.

If you truly know why you're in college, where it can lead you, and find interest and joy in almost every subject, you'll be motivated to work hard. You will be motivated to slog through — and even excel — in classes that may not be your favorites. You'll be motivated to study and step outside your comfort zone for an incredible college experience, because you feel connected and excited by what you're learning and where you're headed.

College should not be something to just get through — it should be an enjoyable, engaging time in your life, every step of the way. I assure you, if I'd chosen a major that didn't work with my interests and personality, I would've missed out on a successful college experience. Don't let anything or anyone else choose your major for you. Choose wisely and enjoy your choice.

Once you've chosen your major, don't forget to connect with other students who are studying the same thing, both at your community college and prospective universities. Build your own learning community, share opportunities, learn from each other, take classes together, study together, engage in similar clubs and interest groups, help each other find internship opportunities, and make the most of college life.

Choosing a major that interests you, excites you, and makes the most of your strengths and talents will lead to improvement in your grades and your overall college success...

- because you will have direction,
- because college will be for you, not for anyone or anything else,
- because you'll be choosing a major for all the right reasons,
- and because you will take control of your life and that feels *great*.

Write it Into Existence

MY GOAL: I am going to major in _____

and transfer to_____

by _____.

For exclusive steps and the best resources for choosing a major, visit

isaadney.com/freestuff

Chapter 6

The New Kid Again

ALEX

"I always advise transfer students to embrace change. Being a transfer student is actually a blessing, because you get the best of two worlds. Instead of being intimidated by the fact that you're a stranger on campus, embrace it as a brand new chapter in life. Join clubs and organizations, gain mentors, make new friends. This is another chance for you to add to your college experience—make it count!"

—Seminole State College of Florida & University of Central Florida

I AM A LATINA country girl. I know I'm not the only one, but I grew up with one side of my family tree stemming from Puerto Rico and New York City, while the other side owned livestock and trucks with tires for driving through mud. I absolutely love both sides, and the eclectic blend of backgrounds at family gatherings was wonderful. But, growing up, I often struggled to identify completely with one culture or the other.

Somehow, I often felt isolated.

That's how you may feel when you attend a community college and then transfer to a university. Your identity is split in half, and you only have a few years at each institution to get engaged, make friends, and take advantage of opportunities. And while you'll want to do what I eventually learned—

embrace both identities and be excited you get two instead of one—you'll still face challenges. Many community college students find that as soon as they start feeling connected, brave enough to take on leadership positions, and comfortable at their community college, it's time to transfer.

It's time to be the new kid again.

This is not a bad thing, but that doesn't mean it's easy. And it doesn't mean you should prolong your community college experience just because you're comfortable there. Transferring to a university is an exciting step—and while it can be a tough adjustment at first, you'll gain the worthwhile and character-building experience of adjusting to a new environment and making a place for yourself wherever you are. This skill will serve you greatly in the long run and make you more prepared for the working world after graduation.

I've talked to many community college students who had a hard time once they transferred to a university. Their difficulties often had nothing to do with classes and coursework. Most students who transfer find they were wonderfully prepared for the university by their community college professors.

What they seem to struggle with is connecting to the large, new social world that's thrust upon them. Transfer students are challenged to make friends with students who've already known each other and lived in residence halls together for the past two years. They are faced with managing another round of college admissions, financial aid, and registration. Students from lower socio-economic classes (like myself) may experience culture shock and find it hard to relate to wealthy university students who wear Lacoste polo shirts and drive BMW's. Often, students like myself can't afford to join sororities or fraternities, which can make it even more difficult to get engaged on campuses where Greek life is the primary source of social connection.

What should you do?

The first step is to connect early with your transfer university. If you wait until the first day you walk onto campus, it will be too late; two years goes by incredibly fast. So, while you're in community college you must begin planning the transfer. Make a list of the top three universities you'd like to attend. I recommend one "reach" school (a college you're not sure you can get into), a second school you're fairly certain you can get into, and a third school where you know you'll be accepted. (See Chapter 10 for advice on how to choose your transfer options.) Once you've established your top three transfer possibilities, begin connecting with those colleges as deeply as you can.

If at all possible, I recommend you visit the college in person, sign up to take a formal tour, and contact the academic department or admissions department to try to arrange an opportunity to attend a class. Sitting in on a class and meeting the academic department chairs of my intended major program was the most impactful experience I had when I chose my own transfer university.

While you're there, eat lunch in the cafeteria. Visit the bookstore. Buy a T-shirt. Ask students who are walking around what they like about the college and what they don't like.

I know this can be expensive if your top colleges are far away, but I believe you need this exposure to make an informed decision. Many students I know made road trips out of the process and traveled with a few friends who were also considering that university. Make it fun and let this experience invigorate, motivate, and excite you for what lies ahead.

In addition to visiting your possible transfer universities early, I recommend doing extensive research on their websites. Find out what classes are required in the major programs you're considering. Read about the professors. Research all the scholarship opportunities and begin developing your community college experience in a way that qualifies you to win them.

Don't forget to also read every line of their student activities page. Study every club and make a list of the ones you find most interesting. Next, write down information for each group and call or email the contact person (usually the club president). Let her know you may be transferring to that college and ask for advice about what the club is like, what she likes best about that university, what she finds most challenging, and then (if you live nearby), ask if you might attend a meeting or an upcoming club event.

Then gather all your courage and go.

Introduce yourself to people and get a feel for the campus culture. If you connect well with students in the club, get their contact info, connect with them on Facebook, and try to meet them again. Having contacts at your transfer university before you move there will be a huge boost for your social life and self-confidence.

The next most important thing you must do for a successful transition is something I skipped: *attend orientation*. I know you may be thinking, "Duh!" But trust me on this. When I got a postcard in the mail inviting me to my university orientation, I glanced at it for a second and thought:

Well, this is probably just for freshmen. I can manage college now and don't need to spend a whole Saturday going through stuff I already know. I got through community college without orientation so why do I need it now?

Worst decision I ever made. And to this day, I truly don't know what I was thinking.

I did meet with my advisor to register for classes, but beyond that, my first transition experience to the university came on the first day of classes.

That day was a nightmare.

I was a commuter, so I drove to campus and circled the buildings, trying to find out where to park. Everything required a parking pass, and I realized I didn't have one. I tried to park in visitors' parking on a narrow, one-way street and almost hit a parked car. I wasn't allowed to park in the visitors' lot, so I had to think of something else. I then grabbed the campus map and looked for parking and security. Tucked away in a small woodsy part of campus I finally found their office and got my parking pass. By a miracle I was able to find a spot in commuter parking and reach my first class in time. The antique building just screamed academia. I was excited for my first class, but looking around, I didn't know anyone—and honestly, it didn't appear anyone cared to know me. I always made friends easily in community college and after the first day of class, people seemed anxious to get to know each other. Not in this class. Some students were in their pajamas. Others had already circled up with their friends from residence halls or sororities.

And I felt, once again, alone. The new kid again.

I realized I would have to make an effort.

So I began exploring how I could get engaged in campus life. Greek life was a big part of the school, but I couldn't afford a sorority and wasn't sure it was right for me. So one night I hung around campus after classes to attend the club recruitment event. I talked to people at every table that interested me and finally clicked with the dance team, the commuters club, and the orientation leaders. I made the dance team, joined the commuter club, and—at the end of the year when it came time to interview orientation leaders—I made the orientation team. These organizations helped me connect with people in common situations, explore interests, and practice my leadership skills.

As a commuter, getting involved can be difficult, as many activities happen at night. However, I was committed to my college experience and often stayed on campus after classes to participate. This was a great way to ensure I was always ahead on my homework assignments, and it gave me a chance to connect with even more people. My university had a commuters' lounge where I was able to spend time; I also got a lot of homework done in the library, and sometimes I would hang out in one of my friends' dorm rooms. (I highly recommend living on or near campus when you transfer—but if you simply cannot afford it, staying late on campus is the next best option. Whatever you do, never just attend classes and go home.)

My favorite experience (and the most ironic) was becoming the orientation leader for transfer students. I quickly realized I had made a huge mistake by skipping my transfer orientation and wanted to make sure no other transfer student missed this opportunity. I called each transfer student a few nights before to make sure they understood how this opportunity would help them get engaged and feel comfortable with everything they needed to know in this new experience.

As a community college transfer student, you definitely know a lot more than a freshman, but every college has a different culture and new procedures you must become accustomed to, no matter what stage of college you're in. And most importantly, when you're new to any situation it's vital to be around others who are also new to connect, engage, and make fast friends.

This chapter is in the Peers section of the book because making friends quickly is essential when you're the new kid again. And I don't mean making friends just to party with—I mean finding people you can learn with, have fun with, and feel connected to. When you make these types of friends, you can experience the joy and growth that only comes from shared experience with people you enjoy. Get engaged early and often, and keep trying different things and meeting a variety of people until you find something or someone that clicks.

Keep in mind, you aren't the only community college transfer student on your new campus who is looking for friends. How can you find each other? Many universities sponsor transfer clubs, commuter clubs, first-generation, and multicultural services programs that are incredible opportunities for connecting with people. Of course, you'll want to make friends with all kinds of students, but there's nothing wrong with finding peers who share your community college background. If you already know people from your community college at your transfer university, don't feel like you have to start over. Likewise, you shouldn't just stick with those friends, but take full advantage of that support group and also feel free to explore the university together and find other friends to join you.

If the university doesn't have an organization that brings together community college transfer students in some way, be the leader who starts one. Go to your student activities office and talk to the staff member in charge of orientation. Find out how you can help create an organization that provides support and friendship for community college transfer students. This may grow into a large club, or it may be small with just a few members. I guarantee it will make a difference in your life and the lives of every person to whom you reach out. If you have an organization like this at your university, or you choose to start one, please tell me all about it at...

isa@communitycollegesuccess.com

And finally, once you reach your transfer university, make it your goal to become the leader of a club or organization on campus. You can choose any group that interests you, but I highly recommend becoming a leader in a club that's either closely related to your major/career or provides leadership skills that will be highly attractive to a future employer. Find something you can use on your resume. I know this seems like extra work and, by the time you reach the last two years of college, you may want to just get in and out. However, you'll end up with job prospects and an enjoyable college experience only if you invest in your final years of college by connecting with peers, exploring your own talents and leadership capabilities, and stepping outside your comfort zone. This will lead to opportunities beyond your wildest dreams. For me, following these steps at my university led to a $2,000 research grant, a trip to New Orleans, a trip to England, a high-ropes-course leadership retreat experience, a $1,000 orientation leader stipend, an award as Top Communications Student, the honor of being a commencement speaker, and a $3,000 top graduate award.

Fully embrace both your college identities and commit to making the most of them. You'll achieve a successful experience and an identity all your own.

For my transfer success checklist and other helpful transfer resources, go to

isaadney.com/freestuff

Chapter 7

The Alumni Advantage

SABRINA

"Making friends in college gives you a support system while you're in school; people who can relate to the stress and joy you go through. And once you leave college, they become a network of friends who can help you find a job. It's also amazing to have people in your life who help you remember where you started and how far you've come."

—Seminole State College of Florida & University of Central Florida

GROWING UP, I never understood the importance of alumni connections. Since no one in my family went to college, no one was ever dedicated to a college sports team or had large networks of friends from their youth. As I grew older, I realized when people found out they went to the same college, they were excited about the connection. They bonded over football pride, hatred of their rivals, and common knowledge of college culture. I always thought these connections were trivial—a quick moment to reminisce about fun times and then move on. I had no idea alumni connections go far beyond rooting for the same teams. I slowly realized people who stay in touch with their alumni associations and college friends have a huge, built-in network that can lead to tremendous opportunities. When you're part of these networks, you, too, will have the opportunity to help others, because people who have the largest networks are usually the ones who seek to help others before themselves. You may think getting ahead in life through your connections isn't fair, and in many ways it isn't—but that's how the world works. People like to deal with their friends. If you've ever led anything, I'm sure you felt the same way. Therefore, the more people you connect with, the more opportunities you'll have. All the secrets in this book are meant to help you take advantage of this human trait and avoid being passed over because you missed the power of connections. The biggest secret, however, is that you should not seek people out *for* opportunities or to *get* something from them. You should seek them out to get to *know* them because you like them or have something in common with them. The opportunities will flow naturally from there.

Unfortunately, alumni associations for community colleges are either nonexistent or not very active. As students transfer to four-year colleges with more robust alumni associations, they tend to identify only with that group. However, as many of my community college friends and I discuss, we often feel a stronger affinity to our community colleges. I hope you'll get involved with your community college alumni association and help it become a more active presence in your two-year college community. A strong alumni association would be beneficial to you and your college for three reasons:

1. An extensive alumni network provides more scholarship money for you and your classmates via alumni donations.

2. Alumni events and contact databases allow you to deeply connect with successful professionals in your area with whom you can form a bond.

3. Staying connected with your community college friends via an alumni network is a great way to maintain a support network and friendships throughout your transfer process and long after graduation.

Talk to your college foundation or alumni association and find out how you can get involved or help create a robust alumni group at your college.

(Note: starting an initiative like this at your community college would make you stand out when applying for scholarships, and if you're at all interested in working in higher education, fundraising, or community relations, being a part an initiative like this is a *great* resume builder.)

Alumni associations are the key to staying connected, meeting professionals with whom you can relate, and building a sense of legacy at your college. Be a part of that legacy.

In addition to becoming involved with your community college alumni association, be sure you connect with your four-year college alumni association as soon as you transfer. When alumni return to campus for homecoming or other alumni events, it's a great opportunity for you to meet people with whom you'll have a lot in common and from whom you can learn. I didn't realize this until after I graduated from my four-year college. My alumni association provided a database of all alumni who were willing to share contact information. I was able to see everyone who shared my major and lived nearby. I had informational interviews with them, and we connected over common professors and college events. They mentored me and gave me invaluable advice. I was amazed at how instantly we clicked just by attending the same university—even though we graduated at different times.

Once you graduate from your two-year and four-year institutions, stay in touch with your friends. The support network they provide is priceless. Also, after you've taken all the advice in this book, shared your incredible talent with the world, and become wildly rich and successful—please donate back to your community college.

Conclusion

I'll never forget the day I won the $110,000 Jack Kent Cooke scholarship, which included $30,000 a year for my bachelor's degree and $50,000 for my master's degree. In an instant I knew my entire life had changed. Not only would I be the first in my family to attain a bachelor's degree, but I would also earn a master's degree. When I stood up to accept the surprise award at the honors graduation banquet, the knowledge of this overwhelmed me, and I instantly fell to my knees and wept on the carpet of the multi-purpose room. What I remember next is that my friends helped me up — and they were crying too. These were friends who needed the money and deserved it as much as I did. These friends cared about me so much and were so happy for me — they cried. Without those friends I wouldn't have had the experience and confidence necessary to win the Jack Kent Cooke Scholarship. That moment will stay with me for the rest of my life. Friends make a difference.

What I miss most about college is getting to be around those friends all day, every day. Embrace this time in your life and make the most of it. Not only will those connections lead you to job opportunities, they will also lead to self-discovery. Some of the greatest epiphanies, the most fun times, and the most memorable moments, will happen among great friends. Choose your friends wisely and realize the people you choose to surround yourself with will have a tremendous impact on your life. Choose people who challenge you to be better. Choose people who want to go far in their lives and who won't let anything get in their way. Choose people who lift you up when you're feeling down and will study with you, encourage you when you get a bad grade, and call you when you're not in class … and have the courage to let go of the friends who don't.

The experiences with your peers in classes and clubs, on trips, in the hallways, and through alumni connections will have an important impact on your life. Cherish the people who support you and believe in your potential to be a leader in college. Your peers will help you grow as a person, learn about yourself, and have the courage to accomplish amazing things. Take advantage of every opportunity to connect with your community college friends, and always be on the lookout for how you can mentor or impact someone else. I believe peer mentorship is one of the most powerful forces available to us. If you're the kind of person who reads this book, I know you're a leader—exactly the kind of mentor other students need. Tell them about this book. Talk to them in class. Invite them to join a club. Ask them to visit a four-year transfer university with you. Go together. Learn together. Thrive together. Succeed together.

Section II—Professors

LINDA

"All my professors and advisers at community college enabled me to make it to where I am today because of their great advice and unwavering support. They taught me to value myself and never give up—two lessons that changed my life forever."

—Miami Dade College &
Georgetown University

Chapter 8

Translators of the College Language

ALEX

"Since neither of my parents earned college degrees or had the financial means to support me, I had to take the initiative to find scholarships, mentors, and community to help me succeed in college. What helped me overcome obstacles was not being afraid to ask for help. I was amazed at how many people were willing to connect me with the resources necessary to succeed in college."
—Seminole State College of Florida & University of Central Florida

FAFSA. Accreditation. Credits. Transcripts. SAT. ACT. GRE. PERT. B.A. B.S. Withdraw. Incomplete. Section 205. MAT 1055. Educational plans. Defer payments. Degree audits. Grad check.

Sound familiar? Sound confusing? It was to me.

Every culture has its own language: a unique way of talking, communicating, and navigating the world. College is its own culture, and when you are the first person in your family to seek a higher education, this new environment can bring about a huge culture shock. The college environment includes nuances you can't find in a book—things you can only learn by talking to those who live within it every day: the college faculty and staff.

Get to Know the Administrative Staff

Most of this section focuses on the incredible relationships you can build with professors and the thousands of dollars in scholarships and opportunities to which those professors will lead you. However, I can't miss an opportunity to mention the advantages I gained by getting to know the administrative staff. Before you can meet a professor or attend class, you must go through each step of the administrative process, including applications, registration, advising, and financial aid. If you've already started college, I'm sure you know what I mean when I say you've been given the runaround (rushing from one department to the next, trying to get something done and not getting anywhere). No matter where you attend college, this seems inevitable. Completing administrative tasks, from financial aid, to registration, to advising can leave you angry, discouraged, and ready to bolt for the front door. Let me share a few secrets for making it much easier.

GARY

"Anything new is always scary and a challenge, but acclimating yourself to the staff and faculty is the best thing you can do to become more confident in your abilities as a student."
—Jefferson College and University of Tampa

College administrative tasks are daunting. I used to work in an admissions office, and I saw firsthand how hard people work to get you into college and how complicated the process can be. Service excellence and ease are important, but most colleges have to follow rules and regulations that can sometimes keep the administrative process from being user-friendly. The college process often isn't easy for the staff or the students. And sadly, when administrative processes go wrong or you forget to do your part, the results can hurt your progress. Recognizing the difficulties is the first step to making it easier.

The first secret is getting to know the people who serve you in administration. You won't have time for a long conversation, but smile, be respectful, and try to see the same person whenever you can. Ask questions. Ask for advice. Ask for a name and use it. Build rapport with people who help you, and return to say thank you when you've successfully gotten into your classes. Many of these workers constantly meet the not-so-respectful students who cause problems and are unappreciative. The successful students are easy to take care of and usually move in and out of their offices quickly. Thus, the workers end up spending most of their time with difficult students and will appreciate and remember your gratitude.

Make a conscious effort to maintain a friendly, respectful attitude and build rapport with those who are working on your behalf. This will bring you more success in registering for classes, working out your financial aid, and all the other administrative tasks that come with college. The kind of students who rant and rave in the office (or on the college Facebook page) will never go as far. This good-guy strategy will save you more time and frustration than you can imagine, and you'll find the people behind the college administrative processes can become incredible connections and resources to help with your college experience.

The key, once again, is: don't be afraid to ask for help. Ask every day. Most people work in colleges because they love helping students. If you ask and then genuinely thank that person, you'll build relationships with knowledgeable people who are glad to assist when the college process seems confusing.

Make a special effort to get to know your advisor and try to see the same one as often as possible. Build rapport with the people in financial aid. Acquaint yourself with the staff in registration, testing, admissions, and other offices. You'll be dealing with these processes throughout your entire collegiate life, and even afterward when it comes time to order transcripts. If you manage this in the best way possible, you'll end up with a large group of people on your team, rooting for you, fighting for you, and teaching you how to manage the administrative intricacies necessary to graduate from college.

These daunting college administrative processes can be a huge barrier for first-generation students and those new to the college environment. Remember, I cried when I began community college—and that happened because I had to wait in the advising office for two hours. The loneliness of the administrative part can be difficult to rise above, but everything changed when the advisor finally called my name, looked me in the eye, and helped me select my first semester of classes. My academic advisors were essential to helping me manage the new process and take the right classes, and I don't know what I would have done without them. They'll become your best advocates if you take time to get to know them, ask advice, and email or come back to tell them how much their help meant to you. The more people you know by name in offices such as advising, registration, and financial aid, the better your college experience will be.

Understanding the college administrative process is a class within itself, so take this seriously, learn everything you can, and get to know the "professors" of that class: the administrative staff. From registering for the right classes, to filling out paperwork so you can graduate, the help and guidance from administrative staff will save you precious time and money.

And the final secret: Read the "textbooks" of the college administrative "class" that most students ignore, such as the college catalog and any emails, letters, and texts you receive. Much of the information and important due dates are there for you, because the administrative staff wants you to succeed. Sadly, too many students skim through this material and later pay the consequences. We're all bombarded with data every day and constantly have to filter out what isn't important. Be careful not to delete or ignore information from your college— it's important.

As you go through the college experience, be your own advocate, double-check your progress every semester on your unofficial transcript, and always check your educational plan with your university plan to make sure you're on the right track. Read everything your college writes to you, and know the administrative staff by name.

For an overview of the most important administrative tasks and definitions, go to

isaadney.com/freestuff

Meet Your Professors

Once you've built the administrative foundation and successfully scheduled the right classes, it's time to meet your professors. While administrative staff will help you get into your classes, professors will help you get A's in the classes and guide you toward incredible scholarships, opportunities, programs, and transfer universities.

The professors in my life helped me get into the honors program, earn straight A's, learn how to write winning scholarship essays, become president of Phi Theta Kappa, choose the right major, travel on my first airplane, get my picture on a college billboard, win the $110,000 Jack Kent Cooke scholarship, win a $2,000 research grant, travel to New Orleans, win a top communications award, get into three honor societies, become the graduation commencement speaker, and win the $3,000 award for the top graduating senior. I tell you this not to pat myself on the back, but to highlight the incredible impact professors can have on your life. All of the above and so much more can happen *for you too* if you invest in getting to know your professors, listen to their advice, and act on it.

Professors know how to succeed academically and are in the profession because they want to teach you what they know. Unfortunately, too many students stare with dead eyes, turn in assignments late (or not at all), and don't go out of their way to interact with a professor unless they're failing a class. When you make the effort to engage with your professors, most will happily lend you their knowledge and want to recommend you for dozens of incredible opportunities you don't even know exist.

This process should begin on the first day of classes. Turn the page, and I'll show you how to make the most of the incredible resource that speaks to you in front of the classroom every day.

Chapter 9

*Getting to Know Your Professors —
The Mystery of Office Hours*

GRACE

"Don't be afraid of getting to class a little early or staying a bit late. Many students are afraid of being alone with their professors, so they won't arrive early, and they rush out as soon as class is over. Honestly, some of the best conversations I've had with my professors have been either before or after class, when no one else was around. This time is precious, so use it to get to know your professor!"

—Seminole State College of Florida

YOUR GRADES ARE the first and most important thing professors can help you with. Most students know this, but unfortunately they take the wrong approach. The first misstep some students make is blaming a professor for a bad grade. How many times have you heard "Ugh, I failed a test. That professor sucks."

Is every professor perfect? Of course not. But is the professor responsible for your grade? Absolutely not. You're the only one who can take responsibility for your grades, and you must do this to succeed.

Regardless of whether or not you like the professor or whether he's doing an outstanding job, you must take control of your grades and work with that professor and his coursework to attain the best possible grade.

MICHELLE

> *"My college English professor gave me the confidence I needed. She challenged all of us and also became my mentor. She convinced me to take on leadership roles, and I even became her work-study student. I wouldn't have been as successful if it weren't for her belief in me. Having her as a support system gave me a true community college experience."*
>
> —Quinnipiac University

The first step to getting good grades is choosing classes and a major that highlight your strengths and interests. Had I taken classes in physics instead of communication, I can almost guarantee I wouldn't have graduated with a 4.0 grade average. Getting to know professors in your introductory classes is especially important, because they can be resources as you research majors. Professors understand academic majors and can help you figure out which will be best for you.

ALEX

> *"I was scared of not choosing the right career path/major. However, the less time I spent worrying about it and the more time I spent figuring out my interests and skills, the more clear my choices became. All I had to do was solidify my thoughts with peers, mentors, and advisors, and I was able to make a well-thought-out decision."*
>
> —Seminole State College of Florida &
> University of Central Florida

Developing a relationship with a professor takes strategic action on your part. Each instructor has a unique personality and way of doing things, so you must be good at reading people and approaching them in a way that suits them best. For example, if you're dealing with a warm and friendly professor, you can start building a mentorship relationship right away. If you're dealing with a professor who's a bit more strict or distant, you'll want to prove yourself by doing well in class and taking it seriously before you approach her. You'll figure this out as you go along.

CYNTHIA

"My math professor showed me I was capable of anything."
—Bronx Community College & New York University

Standing out from the pack and building a relationship can start when you take advantage of office hours. Most professors list their office hours on the syllabus, yet few students understand what these hours are for, or how to use them. Office hours are open times when students can walk in and talk to a professor. This time is invaluable, and you must start taking advantage of office hours as soon as the first week of class. Here's the proven formula that worked for me and dozens of other successful community college students:

1. **First day of class:** Sit in the front row and pay close attention to the syllabus. This is your road map for getting an A in the class. Professors will be peeved if you ask a question that's already answered in the syllabus. Read it carefully the first time and then skim it before class every day.

2. **Second time in class:** Fully participate. Professors know and respect students who look them in the eye, engage in the lectures, take notes, do the reading, attend every class, and speak up during class discussions. If you try to talk to professors during office hours without first showing you're a dedicated student in class, it just won't work. Professors are happy to help students who work hard to help themselves. They're less likely to help if it seems you're trying to get all the answers without doing the work.

3. **Second week of class:** Walk into your professor's office during scheduled office hours (or make an appointment, depending on your professor's preference as described in the syllabus). As you use his name, pay close attention to the syllabus and how he introduces himself the first day of class. If he has a Ph.D, be sure to call him Dr. [last name]. I've had professors who prefer a first name basis, but if they don't clearly specify this, always default to Dr. or Professor [last name]. Shake his hand and briefly introduce yourself, reminding him which class you're taking. If you visited during walk-in hours, ask if this is a convenient time to talk with him for a few minutes. If so, take a seat and begin. If not, ask to schedule another meeting.

4. **First meeting with professor:** During this first meeting, be prepared to ask specific questions and comment on the class so far. Each meeting will be as unique as the student and professor, but here are the main things you may want to talk about the first time:

    a. If this is a class you're good at and interested in, tell the professor how much you look forward to the course content, citing specific topics that will be coming up in the syllabus. Ask him about his degree, where he went to college, and what advice he has for academic success. Don't be afraid to be honest and vulnerable. Don't cry out your life story, but don't be afraid to share your concerns and fears regarding the college experience in a way that shows the professor you're genuinely seeking guidance and not just trying to "suck up." Sucking up never works, and professors see right through it. You must be genuine.

    b. If it's a class you aren't good at or interested in (this should be a required class, because you should never choose an elective/optional class you're not good at or interested in): Tell the professor you want to do well in her class, but you've struggled in the past with this subject. Ask her to share advice on how to succeed and what you can do now to prepare for tests and projects. Ask for additional resources (reading, websites, tutoring, or programs) and how you should follow up when you need additional help. Also ask this professor where she went to college and what advice she has for you in succeeding academically.

5. **Follow up:** After that first meeting, take action on the professor's advice. You should then thank him in person before or after class, or during office hours; let him know you took his advice, and tell him how that advice helped you. This is the most important step. Do not ask anything else at this time. Simply say thank you, and continue showing your interest, engagement, and hard work in the class by following the syllabus, participating in class, and doing all the work to the best of your ability.

6. **Before the first project or exam:** Review the parameters you've been given, start the project (or begin studying), and make a note of any questions, concerns, or problems you're having with a particular area. Once you've done the initial overview, see your professor again during office hours and ask for help with a specific problem or question. Be sure you do this at least a week or two before the project or exam is due, so you don't appear to be a procrastinator asking for help because you didn't invest enough time in the project. Even if you think you know everything and feel prepared, find a question to ask (such as clarification or to ask if you're headed in the right direction with what your paper is going to be about or with particular areas you're studying). For the most part, you should always need additional help with something. The worst mistake students make is not asking the professor for help until they've failed the first exam or project.

7. **After the first project/exam:** Once you get your first graded project, essay, or exam back from a professor, resist the temptation to put it away in a binder never-to-be-seen-or-heard-from again. Read through the graded assignment and carefully review any wrong answers and/or any comments the professor made. Circle or make note of the aspects of the project, essay, or exam where you lost points. Bring that assignment to your professor during office hours to ask specific questions and review why you got certain things wrong. Don't worry about asking questions on mistakes you now understand—focus on things that still confuse you and for which you need further clarification before the next big project, essay, or exam. This meeting does not have to be a long session. Ask the professor to briefly clarify what you did wrong and listen avidly to what he has to say. Don't take it personally, but do take notes and make it a point to apply the constructive criticism to your next assignment. The effort you invest in the beginning will pay off big time when it comes to your final grade—and not because you sucked up to a professor and he gives you a grade because he or she liked you—but because you took the time to make the most of your professor's office hours and expertise, and because you invested yourself fully into doing your best.

As you know, every professor is different. You will love some professors and others not so much. Engage deeply with the few professors you truly like and connect with, but always connect with *every* professor at least once at the beginning of the semester. The only way you'll know which ones you connect with, and can learn from beyond the coursework, is to engage with every single professor. This will not only help you improve your grades, it will also create an invaluable mentoring relationship with a professor and may lead to wonderful opportunities.

Some students have told me they have trouble meeting with professors, as many adjunct professors in community colleges don't have offices or clear office hours. Don't let this stop you. This is not the time to get angry or demand time with your professor. This is the time to get creative. Email the professor. Get to know her before and after class. Ask if you can arrange to meet in a common area (e.g., cafeteria or library) to ask her advice. If you find you're still having trouble or the professor isn't interested in helping you (this is rare but it can happen), be sure to write clearly, honestly, and responsibly about your frustration when it comes time for the course evaluations at the end of the semester. If adjunct office hours are becoming a problem college-wide, don't be afraid to approach your academic administrators or student governments to talk about how the school can better connect students and adjunct professors.

GARY

"I definitely suggest finding one or two professors you love and spending as much time with them in and out of the classroom as possible. The things I learned from one professor here are worth more than the cost of my education."
—Jefferson College & University of Tampa

One of the greatest benefits of community colleges is the close interaction with professors. As I mentioned earlier, community college always felt like a private school education for a public school cost because, for me, the most important benefit of a private school is the small student-to-professor ratio. I attended both a community college and a private university, so I don't know first-hand what it's like to manage in a class of 400 students. I can only imagine connecting with your professor would be much more difficult, but I'm sure it's still possible, so do your best.

Another community college advantage is that most professors choose to teach there because they want to focus more on teaching than research. Take advantage of the time this allows you to spend with your professors. You can (and must) find these connections when you transfer to a four-year college, but starting relationships in community college is vital. Be the student who exposes office hours for what they really are—an incredible time for outstanding students to make the most of their academic success and learn from the brilliant academic minds who teach the classes you're paying for.

What Students are Saying

GRACE

"My professors are some of the most encouraging people I've met. My Oral Communications professor told me how my hard work would turn into success. And my College Success professor encouraged me to join the Honors Program. My professors have helped me to push myself and for that I am so thankful."
—Seminole State College of Florida

VANESSA

"My professors have been my angels. They helped me understand what to do next in my life because they've been there too, and they are always keeping an eye out for me, encouraging me to accomplish great things and keeping me accountable."
—Seminole State College of Florida &
University of Central Florida

For more tips on getting straight A's and strategies to communicate properly with professors, visit

isaadney.com/freestuff

Chapter 10

I Should Just Transfer to the
Closest University, Right?

SARAH

"My main obstacle when trying to enroll in college was not having a mentor. I had no idea how to begin the application process. I didn't know how to apply, nor did I understand the requirements or know if I qualified for the various colleges."

—Seminole State College of Florida

ONCE YOU'VE CONNECTED with your professors and developed the habits of a hardworking and dedicated student, you're ready to ask professors for advice beyond the classroom. I'll never forget the first time a professor looked me in the eye and told me I should and could transfer to *any* university in the country. This was the first time in my life someone had higher expectations for me than I had for myself. As a community college first-generation student, I didn't know a lot about colleges outside my local community. That professor opened my eyes to universities around the country and challenged me to think big. While transferring to the university that's closest to your community college isn't a bad thing (it's probably a great school and many community colleges have partnerships with the nearby university that makes transitioning smooth and easy), it shouldn't be your default choice.

Choosing a transfer university should be a process where you ask for advice, research the best colleges for your major, and determine the ideal fit for you. Most students don't think beyond their local area because—understandably—moving away will cost money. For some students this is reality. If this is the choice you have to make, I know you'll be successful wherever you are. However, many students don't realize they may, indeed, be able to afford a university outside driving distance from home. You can find many resources to pay for college.

Professors opened my eyes to the plethora of opportunities and scholarships out there, as well as the benefits and reputations of different colleges and universities. Sadly, there are many unaccredited colleges that can steal your financial aid, wreck your academic life, and take advantage of students who don't have mentors. Many students don't have the cultural background to decipher these nuances. For example, I met a community college student who was recruited by Harvard during her junior year of high school. She chose a community college instead of Harvard because she'd moved to the United States from Colombia when she was 14. She didn't know what Harvard was and no one told her she was passing up an amazing opportunity.

Once you've established a relationship with a professor you trust, it's time to go deeper to develop a mentorship relationship. Share your academic and career aspirations and ask for advice. If you're uncertain about your goals, then share your confusion and ask for advice. Ask the professor about her academic path and listen for the strategies she used to select a college. Ask what colleges would be best for you with a particular major. This works especially well when you connect with a professor who teaches a subject you want to major in. Share your financial concerns and ask what scholarships are available, as well as what you should do now to qualify for those scholarships. Ask for advice on loans and how to manage your college finances responsibly, while not being afraid to invest in your potential.

Why should you ask a professor for financial advice in

addition to someone in the financial aid office? In my experience, people who work in financial aid don't have time for such candid advice. They can explain processes, but what students need from professors is advice regarding what processes to ask about. Professors are great at encouraging students to invest in their potential and are also highly intelligent when it comes to making smart financial decisions in academia. While professors may not be familiar with updated financial aid or loan regulations, they will often give you great advice about investing in your potential and being smart about how you invest your money in your education and your future.

You'll be amazed at your professors' knowledge and their connections to universities where you will thrive. One of my professors, who knew someone who taught at the university I wanted to attend, drove to the university so I could follow her (I didn't know how to get there or where to park) and then arranged for me to sit in on a class and meet the professor. This was invaluable to me—and it's a perfect example of how professors will bend over backward to help you succeed, if only you ask. But of course, the great secret is this: The more you invest in your own success, the more others will be willing to invest in you. Invest in yourself and ask for help every day. Ask your professors to guide you academically. Ask them where you should transfer, and then take their advice.

Chapter 11

How Professors Helped me Win a $110,000 Scholarship, and How They Can Help You Do the Same

JEREMY

"Knowing a faculty member well enough for that person to write a wonderful letter of recommendation or nomination was key in helping me win awards."

—Pikes Peak Community College & Colorado State University (Pueblo)

IF IT WEREN'T FOR the knowledge, advice, and recommendation letters from my professors, I can honestly say I would never have won over $110,000 in scholarships, transferred to an incredible university, engaged in top-notch honors programs, won incredible awards, or had amazing opportunities to travel. Professors at your community college and four-year university have deep knowledge about their institution's best opportunities and awards. Many of these awards can only be won if you're nominated by a professor. That's why building strong relationships both in and outside of the classroom is so important. Once a professor knows you, sees how genuine and hardworking you are, and believes in your potential, he will invest in you, nominate you, and notify you when awards and opportunities arise. This is where you want to be. This is where the magic happens.

Thousands of scholarships and accolades are available for students who take the time to invest in strong relationships with their professors. You deserve to be one of these students. In addition to building the kind of relationships with professors that will cause them to think of you when these opportunities arise, you also want to make a strong enough impression to elicit a stellar recommendation letter. When it comes time to transfer and apply for scholarships, recommendation letters from professors carry a lot of weight. If you're an average student who makes an average impression on a professor, you'll get—you guessed it—an average recommendation letter. The professor won't have a lot to say about you if you haven't done your part in investing in the class, in the professor, and in extra-curricular opportunities. When you develop strong relationships with professors, the words they write in a recommendation letter can make a significant impact on your life.

KRISTINA

> *"I knew I had to focus in school because it was the only way I could reach my dreams. I had amazing professors who helped me believe in myself. I honestly didn't know I had a lot of potential until one of my professors put me in the Honors Program."*
> —Seminole State College of Florida

When it comes time to ask for these recommendation letters, be sure you do it the right way. Professors are busy and you must give them plenty of time to write your letter. You want a professor to be in the best state of mind in managing her own schedule and in how she thinks of you, so don't make the mistake of asking at the last minute. The rule of thumb is to ask at least two weeks in advance. The best bet is to ask your professor—once you've built a strong enough relationship—how much notice she needs to write a recommendation letter. And once you know it's time to ask for the letter, be sure to provide all the information she needs. Include the following:

- To whom the letter should be addressed.
- The preferred format (e.g., on letterhead, with a signature, sealed in an envelope).
- Where to send the letter when it's completed. Should she email it to you, print it out and leave it for you to pick up, seal it in an envelope, or mail it directly to the college or scholarship committee? If the letter needs to be mailed, provide an addressed and stamped envelope.
- When the letter is due.
- A brief overview of your accomplishments and extracurricular activities. If you have a resume that includes these options, you may attach it as a reference.
- A brief overview/reminder of the class you took with that professor and any special projects you completed.
- A request for her to save the letter in a file so she can simply alter the address and a few other things if you need an additional letter for another opportunity.

Professors are busy, and the easier you can make the recommendation process for them, the better state of mind they'll be in to write the excellent letter you want.

PAUL

"A couple of professors and one adviser mentored me and helped me spread my wings. They have encouraged independent research and networking opportunities."
—Columbus State Community College

Conclusion

Connecting with the faculty and staff at your college, asking for advice, taking that advice, and seeking recommendation letters does require extra work on your part. This calls for organization, persistence, and the will to achieve. The average student just goes to class, returns home, and barely remembers the professors' names. You should never be comfortable with average. You are more than average—you're someone who will rise above the crowd. Invest in your professorial relationships and value everything they offer. They hold the secrets to academic achievement and will help you achieve dreams you may not believe are within your reach.

Your professorial mentors will help you reach higher. They will help you dream bigger. They will help you understand the college world that seems so foreign to so many of us. Embrace these mentors and value their role in your life. They have tremendous power to change it for the better. And all you have to do—is ask.

For more tips on where to find more money for college, visit

isaadney.com/freestuff

Section III—
Professionals

EDWIN

"My friends, advisors, and professional mentors have drawn out the potential inside of me. Through their support, I have received many scholarships and made incredible professional connections that opened the doors of possibility."

—Seminole State College of Florida

Chapter 12

Where Have You Come From, and Where are You Going?

ROSE

"I never saw myself as anything much. And then I met professional mentors who expected me to go farther — and showed me how."
—Seminole State College of Florida & University of Illinois

IF YOU'RE LIKE most people, you may be wondering how connecting with professionals can help you in college. I'm here to tell you this has everything to do with your future. Aren't you attending college so you can find a great job after you graduate?

As I mentioned, I come from a lower-middle class family. Growing up, I never understood class or the cycles of poverty. I assumed if you worked hard, you could make money. I believed if you were smart enough, you'd get to Harvard, but overall, I felt great wealth and success were far beyond my reach and — in fact — it would be selfish and terrible to consider myself worthy of these things. Throughout college, I worked as a nanny and a private tutor. I remember driving through neighborhoods with giant houses, thinking to myself and then later joking with friends — *I just want to walk up and knock on their doors and ask, "What in the world do you do?"* I had no concept of how people made money or why some people have lots of it and others struggle to put food on the table.

My experiences as a tutor also illuminated for me how socio-economic class affects educational opportunities. Some parents paid thousands of dollars to have their kids tutored for SAT, ACT, and AP tests, as well as any subject in which their kid was struggling. I was amazed at how costly tutoring was, how involved some parents were with their kids' education, and that tutoring for college prep tests even existed. When I was a junior in high school, I just showed up one Saturday morning with a pencil and took the SAT, having no idea how important it was to study, or that opportunities were available to invest in studying. The students I met as a private tutor improved their SAT scores exponentially, and for the first time I realized money could buy educational opportunities.

The students and parents I met were wonderful people, and I think it's a fine thing that wealthy parents choose to invest in their kids' education; they want the best for their children, and I admire that. However, it posed a real problem for me. I realized if students who had money were able to get specialized tutoring, support, and guidance from their wealthy and college-educated parents, then students who don't grow up with these benefits have a difficult time competing.

While my parents didn't have the money or knowledge to offer me collegiate or test-prep guidance, I was lucky enough to have the most loving, supportive family in the world. They were willing to accrue hundreds of thousands of dollars of debt for my education. They always praised me when I got good grades, never pressured me, and were proud of everything I did. My mom helped me do science experiments, and my dad helped with my Spanish homework. But as supportive as my parents were, they didn't understand how to guide me in the things I needed to do and learn about college culture. They just didn't know. And I'm one of the lucky ones. I meet so many students who not only lack the financial means for college, but also have parents who don't support their college aspirations.

Wherever you are on the continuum of socio-economic class, the most important thing is to acknowledge this and recognize how it affects where you're going. Then, you must apply what you learn in this book and do everything possible to learn from those above you. Also, don't forget to reach back and help the people behind you, because despite your socio-economic class—or rather, because of it—you deserve an education, and your educational achievement will benefit us all.

While I still don't pretend to fully understand all the issues behind socio-economic class inequalities, I did finally come to understand that your socio-economic background has an impact on your opportunities in life. Whether that impact is positive or negative is completely up to you. I'll show you that what seems like a disadvantaged background may actually become a wonderful resource in your life.

My grandpa from my Puerto Rican side (my dad's father) died this past year and his death made me reevaluate the impact of my family history on my life. Growing up, my grandfather was always just Grandpa to me—the great jokester who always made us laugh, and the guy I thought was the richest man in the world because he gave my brother and me all of the money in his change jar whenever we visited. Not until his death and the evolution of my own understanding did I start to think about the impact our backgrounds have on our lives.

After Grandpa died, I began learning more about his life and the lives and jobs of all my grandparents. The stories came out, and my grandparents evolved from being just "my grandparents" to *people*—real people who came from poverty and did everything they could to create better lives for themselves, their children, and their grandchildren. My mom's dad, one of eleven kids, worked in the military, on train tracks, and—his favorite—for the Department of Transportation mowing lawns on the highways. My mom's mother, who also recently passed away, grew up in a shack in the woods of Tennessee as the youngest of twelve kids. Her father was in and out of jail for selling moonshine and eventually she and her mother moved to Florida. Her mom bought land for $300, grew watermelons on it, drove back up to Tennessee and sold all the watermelon for $300 so she could pay off the land. My grandma lied about her age in order to be a waitress in Florida. When I knew her, she painted, had frequent garage sales, and was always selling her crafts.

My dad's dad (the one who was a janitor from Puerto Rico) was one of thirteen kids. His mom passed away in Puerto Rico from a bee sting; they tried to carry her to the hospital, but it was too late. Afterward, my grandpa's dad told him to never talk about it or cry about it ever again. Before they knew each other, both of my grandparents (my grandma the oldest of nine kids) moved from Puerto Rico to New York because they heard factories were hiring people who didn't speak English—and they wanted to work. My dad grew up speaking Spanish at home and English at school. When he graduated high school he went to community college because he wanted to make money, but he had no idea what to major in or what to do. He majored in business, graduated with his A.A., and got a job right away. He hated his job, and on his first vacation he went to Miami with his best friend and never came back. He worked odd jobs and then met my mom who was just finishing beauty school, and the rest is history. They worked hard to support the family, living in a trailer at one point, doing everything they could to provide for us.

I tell you all this so you'll know why I came to realize that learning from professionals was vital for my success, and why I needed to understand my family history to make sense of my story and to create a solid foundation to continue the legacy of hard work and sacrifice that came before me.

I wanted to break the barriers of poverty and of being a minority, and I wanted to move forward.

My story is one of millions. Every student I've met in community college has an incredible history. Their tales are about overcoming obstacles and fighting to achieve an education. Single moms are trying to make a better life for themselves and their kids. International students struggle to succeed in America. Many students arrive in this country not knowing

English and work harder than anyone I've ever known. Some students come from backgrounds of abuse, or parents who don't support them, or no parents at all. I've listened to students who grew up in deep poverty and hardship, often hearing gunshots outside the front door. I've heard the stories of students who thought about giving up, and the ones who never had anyone in their lives to believe in them.

You have a story, too, and it's important for you to own your story, your history, and your background. Dig into it, uncover the treasures, bury the ugliness, and realize what has given you strength. Understand what parts of your background present barriers in your life, and remind yourself that while sometimes the world is unfair, people can rise above their circumstances and create better lives for themselves, regardless of where they start. The difference in the ones who succeed and the ones who don't, is *deciding* to start and believing you can *finish*.

I encourage you to write your story. Talk to your parents about your grandparents. Think deeply about where you come from and what impact this has on your current choices and opportunities. Think about what kinds of jobs you've been exposed to thus far and what kinds of jobs seem out of reach. Think about what you grew up knowing about college and what you realize you were never exposed to. Appreciate the beauty in your history and understand the barriers. Don't let this fuel anger or hatred toward the inequities and injustice in our world, but instead let your history fuel your desire to invest in your potential through education. Succeed far beyond your family history and use your increased success and power to make a difference for those who still suffer from inequity and injustice. Only you have lived your life, and you are uniquely qualified to understand the problems in your community. Only you can bring the solutions. We need you.

If your family history is anything like mine, then you probably didn't grow up socializing with doctors, attorneys, or CEOs. Most of the people in my family were blue-collar workers, and so when it came to the professional world, I had only the media for guidance. The only jobs I knew of were doctors, lawyers, CEOs, reality TV stars, and forensic scientists. Of course, like most children, I also knew about jobs I saw in my community: teachers, policeman, fireman, superheroes, and princesses. If I could have been anything in the world, I wanted to play Belle from *Beauty and the Beast* on Broadway, but since I could neither sing nor act, I realized this wasn't a smart direction for me to pursue. When it came time for me to choose a major and a job, I thought about the people around me whom I admired and the high school subjects I did well in and decided to be an English teacher. I changed my major and my career choices several times, and my career goals continue to evolve. Ask any adult, and I guarantee most of them will admit they're still trying to figure out what they want to be when they grow up.

The most important point is that my career evolved into something I never dreamed of, thanks to a group of people who expanded my limited viewpoint of the professional world. These people are my professional mentors—incredible men and women who helped shape my career aspirations, and, more importantly, make them reality. I am more thankful to them then they could ever imagine.

The rest of this section will show you how to get high-powered professionals to share their advice with you, become your mentors, and offer you internships and jobs. As a tutor, I learned that wealthy students have these connections built-in; many of them already have internships and jobs lined up before they even start college. These connections are incredibly valuable, but the good news is: you don't have to be rich to get them. You can find them on your own. What you learn from these people can help you choose a great major, land incredible internships, find purpose in your college experience, and create a pathway for incredible professional success.

Chapter 13

The Best Way to Discover Your Perfect Career
(and Avoid a Miserable One)

CYNTHIA

"*Informational interviews are always helpful and they give you insight into what you'll be doing. When I met a speech language pathologist, it confirmed that this was the career for me.*"
—Bronx Community College &
New York University

OKAY, I HAVE TO be up front with you. There's no such thing as a perfect job. I know, my chapter title seems misleading, but there are many people who love their jobs. You'll also meet people who don't love their jobs, but perform with excellence and find joy in that; or people who love some things about their jobs and dislike others. The lucky ones find a passion in life and find a perfect job to fulfill their needs.

For the most part, a job will never completely fulfill you. You have an incredibly unique package of personality, interests, values, skills, and talents, and it's unlikely any job will be an *exact* match. How do I know? Because jobs are a direct result of our economy and the times we live in. My career options 100 years ago would be vastly different than the ones I have today—and the career options I'll have 20 years from now may drastically change. In our rapidly evolving technological world, old jobs disappear and new jobs are created every day. We no longer live in a time where you can stay with the same job at the same company for thirty years. Most people change jobs often and even switch careers as our economy evolves. Too often, people find themselves unemployed and need to learn new skills to fit into the new economy.

In such a rapidly changing world, the only way to prepare yourself to succeed and find the best *kinds* of jobs for you is to…

1. Develop your critical thinking, communication, and creativity skills by dedicating yourself to your college classes and taking leadership positions in extra-curricular activities.

2. Get to know a wide variety of professionals who have jobs that interest you in order to learn what they do and whether you'd like to do that, too.

Even if you grew up knowing many professionals in your life, most students still have no idea what positions are out there. There's no way to keep up with them all, because new job titles are created every day. The only way to understand the variety of jobs you might enjoy (and their corresponding majors) is to talk to people who are doing them right now. Even if you have absolutely no idea what career you want, meeting people with jobs that interest you in any way should help you discover common threads that will clarify your search.

So while there's no such thing as a perfect job for you, there is a way to find the best career path to fit your personality, strengths, interests, skills, and talents.

You can discover a career path that suits you well and brings satisfaction to your life, and community college is the perfect place for you to begin exploring. College is filled with a variety of opportunities, resources, and services that will help you get to know yourself, engage with professionals, and figure out what you'd like to do for forty hours per week in your future. Too many people today are downright miserable in their day-to-day jobs. Life is too short and forty hours a week is too long to truly hate your job. The truth is, as you get older and gain more responsibilities, making big career changes can be difficult. You're wise to do your research while in college and find the absolute best fit in the job market. Connecting with professionals now will make all the difference in giving you a realistic perspective.

A combination of understanding yourself and learning about jobs from professionals will set you up to find (or create) the career of your dreams. Now is the time to begin developing relationships with professional mentors, similar to the relationships you forged with your professors.

As a student, I grew tired of hearing about the "real world" everyone kept saying students don't know about, but I've come to realize what people really mean when they tell us, "Get ready for the real world." They want to try and prepare students for the *professional* world. Every stage of life has its own culture, with rules, responsibilities, and nuances that can make you feel like a small fish in a big pond. The best way to understand the professional world is to speak with the big fish while you're still in college, before you graduate and feel like a lost, post-graduate minnow.

D ANIELA

"*Informational interviews helped me plan my future and identify the best path toward achieving my goals.*"
—Baltimore City Community College & Johns Hopkins University

Informational interviews are an excellent way to start. They changed my life and made possible everything I'm doing right now. I wouldn't be where I am today if I hadn't read the career books that ended up introducing me to the concept of the informational interview. I didn't discover this until after I graduated college and was struggling to find a job. I wish I'd understood this concept while I was still in school, because it would have saved me a year and a half of heartache, depression, and anxiety after graduation. It would have prevented an identity crisis that led to me hastily chopping off my long hair I loved so much. That's why I believe this section is so important—it's what I didn't do in college and wished I had.

CHRISTOPHER

"Informational interviews are an exceptional way to test-drive a career. You can learn about the day-to-day operations of a job, the workload/ expectations, and more about the little-known realities of the position/industry."

—Rochester Institute of Technology

Even though I had great college success, I still found myself unemployed after graduation. Doing informational interviews the way I show you in this section helped me get on my feet, find a job, and eventually learn how to write a book and achieve some of my biggest dreams by the age of 25. I only wished I'd started sooner.

Do not wait until you find yourself graduated and jobless to start doing informational interviews.

Informational interviews consist of asking someone to share information and advice about what he does every day. You can learn more than you ever realized by asking people the questions I'll share with you. While I think it will be incredibly beneficial for you to ask these questions of high-powered professionals in high-powered places, I believe you can learn just as much by asking new professionals and anyone in the world you admire and would like to be someday.

If you want to be a mom one day, then do an informational interview with someone who's a good mom. If you want to be a high-powered CEO, what better way to learn how to get there than learning from other CEO's? The possibilities are endless. I believe the absolute best way to learn anything in life is to ask advice from people who've done what you want to do. The old-time concept of young apprentices learning from master craftsmen was right on. Ask people how they got where they are today and what advice they have for you. Soak it all up!

This knowledge, coupled with the skills you learn in college, is the key to putting you on the path to success.

Doing informational interviews as early as possible will also help you discover a major that fits your strengths and interests and help you find clearer direction and purpose for your college life. You'll gain a mentor who believes in you and challenges you to greater heights, and you'll learn about opportunities and jobs you never knew existed. You'll also get hired for internships at organizations you'd love to work for one day, and you'll develop connections to help you land a job once you graduate.

Let me show you how easy it is to seek out and start relationships with people who will change your life.

What Students are Saying

JESSICA

"After taking Isa's advice about informational interviews, I was soon given opportunities to learn about my dream job—an event planner for Disney. I was able to interview the director of events for Disney World. I got to job-shadow him at some incredible events, which made me even more eager to achieve my goal of being an event planner. And now I have experience and an incredible mentor."

—Seminole State College of Florida

ALEX

"I got a full ride First-Generation Student scholarship at my community college and university. Because of this scholarship, I haven't had to pay one cent of my college tuition. I attribute my success to the close bond I developed with my mentor at the Career Development Center, who told me about the opportunity the first minute she heard about it."

—Seminole State College of Florida & University of Central Florida

Chapter 14

The Value of a Professional Mentor

CHRISTOPHER

"I've learned so much from my mentor relationships. They've built my network and taught me life lessons that are valuable for years to come."

—Rochester Institute of Technology

WE'LL TALK LATER in this section about how informational interviews with professionals can lead to job offers; however, I believe mentorship is the most valuable aspect of informational interviews with professionals. You'll find many definitions of mentorship, but to me mentors are the people in your life who encourage, expect, and expose. Mentors *encourage* you to do more, *expect* you to be more, and expose you to what *more* is. Professional mentors will share priceless advice and expose you to what you need to do right now to prepare for what you want in your future. They will also give you invaluable advice that only comes from experience. Professional mentors can help review your resume, give you interview techniques for your industry, share internship opportunities, and provide online resources that give you further guidance. They also offer places to look for jobs and internships and teach you insider secrets of their particular field and industry.

More than anything else, they will teach you about success, yourself, and how to reach your dreams.

Though I didn't start formal informational interviews until after I graduated college, I did begin the informational interview process with my career counselor and the communications manager at my community college before I even knew what informational interviews were—and these people are still valuable mentors in my life. However, once I graduated with my bachelor's degree and found myself unemployed, I felt lost. I hadn't connected with my community college for over two years, and after a short experience working for an educational company that wasn't right for me, I wasn't sure where I fit.

So the first thing I did was return to the resources of my community college career center. I used their online mentorship site and was able to search for professionals who were willing to serve as mentors to college students.

Hint: if you haven't realized it yet, these career centers are among the most important resources on campus, yet many students don't take advantage of them. Don't let another day go by without using everything they have to offer.

As a new graduate with a B.A. in communications, I found someone who worked in a field many people said I would be good at—public relations. Using the "awesome" context clues I talk about in Chapter 5, I thought, *Yeah, I like to "relate" with people (i.e., the public) so public relations might be perfect for me. There's nothing I love more than being around lots of people and sharing information that can help improve their lives - yes!*

Later, I realized being a public speaker, trainer, and writer was the best fit for me—and that came from many informational interviews, trial and error, and the persistence of always chasing the good feelings that come when you're doing something you love. I love being around people and helping them make their lives better—but I had no idea how my strengths and talents translated into a career. As I continually got to know my strengths and went on informational interviews, my career evolved into something incredible. Get to know yourself, what you love, and when you feel most alive, and never stop chasing that feeling.

So, at the time, I thought public relations might be a good fit. I emailed the professional—Larry Humes—and asked if he'd meet with me for 15 minutes to share his advice and expertise. Larry said yes and invited me to meet with him at his office. From Larry, I learned public relations included a lot of journalistic-type writing (press releases), and I knew that wasn't the kind of writing I most enjoyed. In addition, one aspect of public relations requires skill in crafting specific messages and handling mishaps to protect an organization's reputation. I knew—and could feel as he explained what the field entailed—that it wasn't quite right for my personality and strengths. For most informational interviews, this would be enough and a huge success—I figured out what I didn't want to do before I was stuck having to do it every day. However, it didn't end there. Larry took an interest in me because I did something not many young people do—I reached out to learn from those above me. Larry was impressed.

I recently met with Larry again, some three years later, and he told me, "You know, you're the only student who ever contacted me from that mentorship database." I told him—I hoped that will change after students read this book. By meeting with professionals, you will stand out in their eyes and win their unwavering guidance and support.

As I eventually learned, *everyone* will be impressed if you do the things I teach you in this section. Once they're impressed with you and see you genuinely want to learn and succeed, they'll do everything in their power to help you. That help *will* change your life. There's no way it won't, and it won't always be about getting you a job. It will often be much more than that.

Larry was my first professional mentor after I graduated, and he will always be the person who showed me what professional mentorship looks like. He showed me that wonderful people in the world are willing to share their expertise and be a guiding light for those of us who feel blind and lost in the muck of a post-graduate identity crisis—and those who grew up with little professional guidance in our lives. In addition to Larry's kindness in opening my eyes to the possibilities of mentorship that led to the inspiration for this book, he also became a person I could talk to as I managed the unemployment process. After that first meeting, I kept up with Larry via email. I would tell him how I'd taken his advice, update him on how I was doing, and ask general questions about surviving in the new professional world I found myself in. Larry's emails were a source of comfort and guidance that helped me navigate the new terrain of the professional world. His emails always contained small nuggets of advice I still treasure to this day. Some of the insights Larry taught me include...

- Never be afraid to put your job on the line for something you believe in. Take risks and don't let anyone shut down your fire and ambition.

- Larry introduced me to the most influential book in my life: *How to Be Like Walt* by Pat Williams. Walt's life, creativity, ambition, optimism, and ability to dream big and remember the child in us all inspired the way I approach almost everything I do in my work. The author, Pat Williams, expressed Walt's life in the form of lessons that deeply impacted me. Lesson one in *How To Be Like Walt* helped alleviate my anxiety over finding the perfect job as soon as possible; it was simple but had a profound impact on me: "live the adventure."[6]

I was so stressed about finding a job and the ideal career path that I had forgotten to have fun. I forgot to enjoy the journey. I forgot that life should be joyously chased after, pushed to the limits, and explored. It isn't always perfectly planned—it's often an adventure, and that was something I should embrace and not stress about.

I share these life lessons with you so you can see how deeply one person impacted my life. What Larry exposed me to and instilled in me will always be a huge part of my life. The value of mentorship has no price. It's as unique as the person you

---

6   Williams, P., and Denney, J. (2004). *How to be like Walt*. Deerfield Beach, Fla.: Health Communications. Pg. 15

meet. It's as valuable as that person's life, because mentorship is the time someone takes to share life and wisdom with you. That is something to be sought after and treasured—something we need more of in our world.

I could write an entire book about every mentor in my life who helped me achieve my dreams. Since I don't have room in this book, I will tell you this—I can honestly trace *every* success in my life thus far to a person who made a difference for me: one encounter. One piece of advice. One shift in perspective. One new tool. One new resource. One new contact. One new mentor. Mentorship changes everything and creates new paths along your adventure trail, opening your eyes to things you didn't know existed. It changes, inspires, and motivates you. It leads you to places you didn't think you were worthy of. It leads you to believe you are capable of more. The value of mentorship is that it makes your life *better*.

The good news is: more people than you realize are willing to mentor you—mentoring a student who wants to succeed and takes your advice is one of the best feelings in the world.

Your mentors will cherish you as much as you cherish them.

In the next chapter, I'll share how professional mentors can also lead to job opportunities by accessing the hidden job market and getting incredible internships. While gaining job opportunities from professional mentors is a fantastic benefit, as you seek out these connections always remember that, more than a job, nothing is more valuable than the time a person gives you.

Chapter 15

Okay, Hidden Job Market:
"Ready or Not, Here I Come!"

MARIE

"When I graduated college, it was so hard to find a job. I applied to hundreds of jobs online but didn't hear anything back. I wondered ... where are all the employers I was promised would want me once I had a college degree? It turned out the jobs weren't being filled online."

—Seminole State College of Florida &
Stetson University

DID YOU KNOW 80 percent of all jobs are never posted online? Those 80 percent make up what's known as the hidden job market. Recently, NPR.com did an interview with Matt Youngquist (president of Career Horizons), who confirmed that in the hidden job market, jobs are all filled by "friends and acquaintances hiring other trusted friends and acquaintances." Is this unfair? Maybe a little. Will it change? Probably not. Why? Because in a world filled with much uncertainty, trust is huge. Most people will always want to hire people they already know and trust. That's part of human nature.

So guess what—the more people who know and trust you, the more likely you are to get a job. Most of the time you spend searching online, posting your resume, and blindly submitting your standard cover letter and resume will be a waste. Youngquist said that to get a job, seekers should make about one hundred contacts per month! Sound crazy? That's the reality of the world we live in today—and the sooner you understand and acquire the skills to make professional contacts, the better. You'll need skill and courage, but the earlier you start, the easier it will be. In addition to gaining invaluable mentors, the benefits are huge. In many cases, finding professional mentors and contacts is the *only* way to get a job. The same is true for internships.

Internships are a great way to build relationships with professionals and pave the way for a future job. To get my free mini ebook on how to get the best internships, go to

isaadney.com/freestuff

As I mentioned earlier, I didn't realize how important informational interviews were until I was unemployed and realized that—despite our technological world and the millions of jobs online—getting a job rarely happens on the Internet. Even the 20 percent of jobs posted online are often filled by trusted friends and referrals. Making connections and contacts with people in your industry, and in companies you'd be interested in working for, will change your life and open doors to opportunities that—if you don't have those connections—will remain tightly closed. The hidden job market can either be a source of frustration, or a rich reservoir from which you can draw incredible opportunities from the guidance of those you have succeeded before you.

Now the question is, how do you find these people who will help you discover exactly where 80 percent of the jobs are hiding? The good news is, there are many ways to find them. You just need to know where to look and how to ask.

Chapter 16

Who Should You Talk To, and
Where Do You Find Them?

CHRISTOPHER

> *"Social media is the hub within which success can be accentuated and leveraged. Utilize and expand your network every day, and it will pay off big time!"*
>
> —Rochester Institute of Technology.

WHILE CAREER ADVISORS are saying you should make about one hundred contacts per month to find a job, you may be running scared, wondering how in the world you can find the right people, much less have time to meet them. The good news is: if you're still in college and not looking for a job right now, you don't need to worry about making one hundred contacts per month (though of course, it couldn't hurt). While in college, your minimum goal should be to have at least one 15-minute— in-person or phone—informational interview per month.

Once you get to your senior year, I recommend doing one 15-minute informational interview per week—especially in your last semester. If you're unemployed after graduation, increase your frequency so you're having informational interviews a few times a week until you find a job. Once you have a job, I recommend you continue doing informational interviews at least every other month. I still do them at least twice per month.

The next two chapters will teach you step-by-step how to set these up. The more the better of course, but the minimum should be one per month. This formula will change your life and exponentially increase your job and internship prospects.

The first step is to uncover the kind of people you need to meet. Advice from a professional in any career is enlightening, but to make the most of your time and effort, it's best to focus on meeting people in jobs or industries that interest you. If you're not sure what kind of job you want, that's okay—starting somewhere with *someone* will make a difference and help you clarify your career aspirations. However, if you haven't already done so, read Chapter 5 of this book and visit your career center ASAP to further spell out your direction. Once you narrow your interests, you're ready to start making connections with people who can guide you on the path to success.

The next step is to locate email addresses for people you'd like to meet. I recommend using a simple chart to keep track of the emails you collect and the people you contact.

You can download my free template at

isaadney.com/freestuff

The easiest way to find contacts is asking friends and family if they know anyone in a particular company or job you want to learn more about. A referral from a trusted friend is always best. However, not all of us are already connected to professional people we'd like to learn from, so finding emails and making connections requires creativity, which can also be fun.

You *can* meet these people even if you don't have pre-existing connections. Below are the best methods I've found so far to secure the contact information you need for setting up your informational interviews:

- **College Directory:** Start with your college staff directory. Colleges are intricate and diverse organizations with more jobs than you realize. My first mentors came from staff who worked in my college. Most colleges have employees in a wide variety of jobs, such as business, public relations, marketing, information technology, software development, multi-media, photography, graphic design, human resources, government relations, law, counseling, event planning, international relations, athletics, student affairs, finance, fundraising, non-profit, and of course, professors who are knowledgeable in a wide variety of subjects and industries. Start with your college departmental directory or a trusted college staff member to help you locate people who work at your college in jobs that interest you.

- **LinkedIn:** After you've created your LinkedIn profile (which you've already done, right?), use the search option to review resumes of people who work in your desired industry. You can start searching jobs in the industry by typing a key word or two in the "job title" section of the search. I recommend searching first in your local area and then branching out nationally. The key in this search is to notice what companies people in your desired industry work for. Once you make note of these firms, find the company websites and search their directory, their Contact Us page, or their About Us sections to find specific email addresses. If you can't locate them that way, try to connect directly via a LinkedIn request.

- **Company Websites:** If you already know of a company or type of business you'd like to work for, go directly to the website and see if you can find email addresses for any professionals you admire. This can be simple or a bit difficult, depending on the industry you're interested in and how easily people in that profession want to be found. Do not give up—there is *always* a way. This is where you get to be creative. Once I guessed a professional's email correctly by using a few varieties of her first and last name@companyname.com.

- **Career Center/Alumni Association:** See if your career center or alumni association has a mentorship database. Search the database for people who interest you.

- **Twitter:** Search possible job titles that interest you on Twitter and follow those people. Notice what they say, re-tweet some of their messages if you like them, and eventually work up to making personal contact.

- **Facebook:** Post on Facebook: "Anyone know anyone with a job in [insert desired job/industry here]? I'm looking to learn from a mentor in [insert desired industry here]." People will respond if they know someone.

- **StudentMentor.org:** Search for a career mentor by signing up with the amazing and free StudentMentor.org, and be sure to follow up often with your mentors.

- **Business Cards:** Whenever you attend a conference, hear a speaker, or volunteer at an event, be sure to exchange business cards with people you admire. You can get your own simple business cards for free at many business card websites, such as vistaprint.com. The business cards you receive at these events will, of course, have contact info.[7]

- **Professional Associations:** Join a professional association in your industry. Almost every industry has one. Just search the name of your industry or major and "professional association" and you'll probably find something. If you aren't sure, ask your career center. And then—*join the professional association.* Most professional associations charge a small fee to join so they can hire staff to provide all the great benefits. The good news is: student membership is often incredibly reduced (around $35 to $100/year). While I know for some any amount is a lot, this is one of the best investments you can make for bringing money into your future. Membership gives you access to the general meetings (attend!), mentorship programs, and—the

---

7   Two of my students who always volunteered for events gave me this idea. One—who wanted to be a lawyer and a judge—volunteered at a foundation fundraiser and turned a business card exchange into a lunch with, you guessed it, a judge. Another turned a business card exchange into an internship with the engineering company he longed to work for. All they did was follow up via email asking for advice.

COMMUNITY COLLEGE SUCCESS   115

best—a membership database listing names and email addresses of people who belong to the association. This is the single best place to find mentors. It is completely worth the money and by far the easiest way to find contact information for hundreds of successful and well-connected people in your desired industry.

- **Current Jobs/Internships:** If you already have a job (even a small part-timer) or internship in your desired industry, then you have a great resource for contacting people you admire. Search the company directory and/or ask around to get introduced to people you'd like to meet within the organization. [8]

More than anything, you need creativity and resourcefulness. I made my favorite creative contact through guessing a sports PR guy's email address by using a few combinations of his first and last name@nameofhisportsteam.com. We had a great meeting. The best way to stay on top of your search is to get creative, ask for help constantly, and become super good at using search engines and navigating company websites. The best way to learn? Practice. Practice. Practice.

And finally, remember that your goal in getting these email addresses is not to send a big spam email asking these people to talk to you or find you a job. Each contact must be someone you genuinely admire, someone you're interested in learning from, and someone who has a job you sincerely want to learn about. Each email address will be a key to unlocking the knowledge and the life of a valuable person. If you don't handle email addresses with care, you'll end up in the spam folder, but there is a way to stand out, get responses, and convert those responses to in-person or phone meetings. Let me show you how.

---

8   Another successful community college student taught me this one: She wanted to be an event planner for Disney and got a job working quick-service food in order to learn more about the company. She told her manager she was interested in being an event planner and asked for advice, which led to getting to job shadow and being paid to help at events such as a surprise proposal in the Cinderella Castle, a special culinary event at EPCOT, and an after-hours Animal Kingdom bash.

For a helpful template to keep track of all your professional contacts, visit

isaadney.com/freestuff

Chapter 17

The Magic of Advice–
How to Get Anyone to Talk to You

ERICA

"At first I was frightened to talk with professionals—I figured they wouldn't want to waste their time with a community college student. But they were more than happy to give advice and have been there for me throughout my journey."
—Seminole State College of Florida & Florida State University

SO NOW YOU'VE found exactly who you want to talk with. This person has a job you'd die for, and you truly admire what he does. You have the name, an email address, and *one* shot at making a connection. Scared? Intimidated? Don't be! Remember, it's lonely at the top, and nothing makes people feel more valued than having someone listen to and act on their advice.

How do I know? Because I'm a mentor to college students, and there is nothing in the world I love more.

And I'm not alone in that feeling.

The key to connecting with professionals is remembering you're there to make them feel good and *it's all about them.* This interview isn't about getting a job (though often that can happen) or collecting another business card. It truly is about connecting with another person and making him feel important.

Your admiration and eagerness will make this person feel great about his career and his ability to share that experience. What is success if you can't share it? People want to share and are waiting for someone like you to ask. So now is your chance.

Before I give you the basic strategies, remember these important points:

1. Professionals are busy.

Professionals with jobs are incredibly busy. Many are overworked, overwhelmed, and barely have time to complete all the projects on their plate and manage their personal lives. That doesn't mean they don't have time, or won't make time for you, but you have to remember that because they're so busy, you'll need to stand out for them to take notice.

2. Professionals can smell a job hunter a mile away.

In an economy where people are desperate for jobs, professionals will know if you're slyly trying to meet with them just to get a job. While the ultimate goal is for these strategies to help you find a job, if that's your only goal *it will never work.* You will come off as insincere and no one wants to make time for that. So your ultimate and only goal to have in mind when connecting with a professional is to *learn.* The desire to learn comes before the job. Most people get this backwards.

3. Professionals are people.

Of course professionals are people, but I know when you're a college student, they seem much more than that. They appear scary, successful, and intimidating, and you think they only care about money and business and "professional" things— whatever that means. The truth is, professionals are people just like you who have emotions and a desire to connect. So while it's important to be professional, too often students think being professional means acting stuffy and hiding their true selves. Nothing could be further from the truth. Truly successful professionals are those whose work is a reflection of their greatest personality traits. So when approaching a professional for advice, just be yourself. They will react and connect to *you* and never to someone you pretend to be. And remember, you're impressive because of who you are. Trust me; they will recognize that.

Now that you know the general tone you should cultivate before you write your first email requesting a meeting with a professional, you need to follow a precise formula to get people to respond. As an example, read the email below I sent to a successful college blogger and author I greatly admired, right after I started my blog (CommunityCollegeSuccess.com). I didn't know her at all.

Subject: My hero

Hi Lynn,

I titled this email *"My hero"* because it was the first thing that came to mind when I read your website. I am a recent first-generation college graduate trying to create new paths and find my place in this big world. As a first-generation college graduate, it is hard to find professional women I admire who do something similar to what I want to do. My dream and goal is to be a speaker and author dedicated to community college students and first-generation college students. I really admire your blog and the solutions you bring. I just started my own blog this week, www.communitycollegesuccess.com, and would love to ask your advice.

I wonder if you wouldn't mind speaking with me on the phone for 15 minutes to share advice on what it takes to be a successful speaker and author in higher education? I rarely meet anyone like you, and it means more to me than you know to be able to learn from successful women like yourself. Would you be willing to speak to me on the phone for 15 minutes in the next few weeks to share your experiences and advice? If so, let me know what days and times typically work best for you.

I really appreciate everything you do and will be keeping up with your blog.

Sincerely,

Isa Adney
isa@communitycollegesuccess.com
555.555.5555
www.communitycollegesuccess.com
http://www.linkedin.com/in/isaadney

Lynn responded within days and our phone conversation directly led to this book you're reading. Lynn's tips gave me opportunities to write for *USA Today College*, which in turn gave me the credibility for publishers to take notice of my book. One person's advice can change your life forever. Reaching out to professionals will lead you on an endless and exciting adventure toward discovering unbelievable opportunities.

While the previous email is a genuine message sent to a stranger, it's also much more. Behind it lies a strategy you can use to get responses from people who can help change your life. If you read it closely, you may even discover those strategies for yourself. But for those of you who need a little help, let's review. (Note: while the themes below are organized in paragraphs, keep in mind an email paragraph should be only two to four sentences in length. Remember, professionals are busy, so the faster you get to your point, the better. Brevity is effective.)

The Intro—"How much I admire you."
The introduction should be easy because you're seeking connections with people who are doing what you want (or at least think you want) to do with your life. Thus, you should genuinely admire them. If not, you're trying to connect with the wrong people. Trying to praise someone you don't actually admire will come off desperate and insincere. So when you begin your email, tell the person what you truly think about her. Show you've done your research and know who she is and what she's accomplished.

Paragraph 2—"Who I am and why this would mean so much to me."

Your email should give a sense of who you are, and I don't mean telling your life story or rambling on about what you're dealing with in your life. You should, however, offer key identifiers that show you deserve advice and you're seeking it with true sincerity. For example, one of my key identifiers is being a first-generation college graduate. When I seek professional advice from a woman, I let her know my mom didn't work outside the home, and thus I appreciate the advice of a successful professional woman. Another key identifier is that you're a community college student seeking advice. If you're the first high school graduate in your family, mention that. If you come from a family with a single mom or a single dad, grew up with your grandparents, grew up in foster care, or recently came to this country, mention that. Mention anything that sets you apart, anything that shows professional advice isn't something in your own backyard. Some of you may have a hard time doing this initially because you may feel you're exploiting your hardships. Perhaps you're proud of where you came from and feel strong because of it. I felt the same way, and this is a good thing, but you don't want to let that unique blend of humility and pride hold you back from sharing your distinctive story and allowing you to get you what you deserve. People will connect with your back-story and key identifiers, so use them.

Other key identifiers include a brief example of your intended major or career goal and how you got interested in this person's profession. The most important thing is to reveal something unique about you.

Paragraph 3—"What I want."

This is where you tell the professional person you'd like to gain advice because you admire him and want to learn from him. You'll notice in the example email, I asked for a 15-minute phone call. Fifteen minutes should always be used for an initial meeting, because most people can find a spare fifteen minutes (for very high-powered professionals, sometimes I only ask for ten minutes). Only request a phone call if the person isn't within driving distance. Meeting in person is always the best and ideal scenario because you will make a deeper, more long lasting connection.

Let the professional know you want to meet with him for 15 minutes for advice about what it takes to be successful in his field. Be as specific as possible and be sure to replace "field" with whatever it is he does. After you come up with your key identifiers and practice writing this email, you'll have a general template you can use over and over again, However, every email you send should be different when it comes to telling professionals why you admire them.

Paragraph 4—Genuine appreciation.

Your closing should be short and to the point, showing genuine appreciation for what the person does. You should already appreciate the work he does, otherwise you wouldn't be interested in doing it yourself. Often people work hard every day without being appreciated, so take this moment to let your contact know you recognize and are thankful for the contribution he makes in the world. Then close by saying you look forward to hearing from him and getting his advice.

While I encourage you to create your own template based on who you are and what you want to learn, on the next page is a guaranteed model (with my notes in italics) to get you started. The key to making this work is infusing it with your personality, style, and sincerity.

Subject: Advice?

Hi Julie, [*I like to use first names, but I also started doing this after I graduated college. This is up to you and what you feel comfortable with and what you feel is appropriate for the particular person you're seeking advice from. If she's within ten years in your age-range, I would use the first name as it is more personal. If not, you may want to consider Mr. or Ms.*].

My name is _____ , and I admire the work you do in *[add specific details about what the person actually does].* I found you by *[say briefly how you found her, whether on their company website, a mutual friend, LinkedIn, you saw her speak somewhere, etc. People like to know how you discovered them, and it increases the sincerity of the approach. Then insert things about the person you admire and are impressed with. Be specific and genuine.]*

I am a_____*[Insert your key identifiers and other personal things about you that show you are genuine and don't have a lot of professional guidance in your life].*

It would mean a lot to me to learn from a successful person like yourself. Would you be willing to meet with me *[or talk with me on the phone]* for 15 minutes and share your advice and what it takes to be successful in *[insert industry/career]*?

Thank you so much for all you do *[in a certain industry, for a certain group of people, etc. Be specific about how her work contributes to the world].* I look forward to hearing from you.

Sincerely,

Your Full Name

Student *[if you hold an office in a club, you can mention that here, such as SGA Vice President]*

Name of Your College

Email *[your email must be professional—I recommend your first and last name]*

Phone

LinkedIn Profile Link

The best way to approach a professional is by having her email address (besides meeting her in person, of course). However, if you use all the techniques in the prior chapter and still can't locate an email address, you may also try to connect via LinkedIn. The only way to do that is to add the contact to your network, and you're only allowed a limited number of words to convince a stranger to add you. Once they do so, you can usually see their email addresses or message them directly. That's when you need to use the above template. To get the initial connection you will click "Connect," on that person's LinkedIn profile, click "friend" as the option of how you know him or her, and then in the message type something like this (do not use the default message):[9]

Hi *[insert name here]*, I am a first-generation community college student *[or whatever your key identifier is]* and really admire what you do *[replace with what they actually do, be specific and succinct]* and would love to learn from you.

Sincerely, Isa/555.555.5555 *[you do not have to share your phone number if you're uncomfortable, but I find it important to show I'm a real person who trusts them and is willing to connect]*.

Since the LinkedIn request is just to get your foot in the door and find a way to directly message this person, you just have to show enough sincerity and explain your intentions to get the professional contact to accept your request. Once she accepts, you will need to email or message her again using the longer template to request a 15-minute phone call *or* an in-person meeting if she's willing.

This artful communication works off a social scientific principle I have discovered: *People love to give advice and love to be appreciated.* If you give that to someone, they will want to bestow wisdom on you, because they see you're sincerely interested. Everyone wants to leave a legacy and feel the life experiences they've gained can help someone else. So make people feel important and soak up all their advice. This is the ultimate key to your success, but you'll never have access to that advice unless you master the art of asking for it.

Practice using the template above with one of the contacts you found from the previous chapter. Before you send the message, have someone (such as a career center advisor)

---

9   Please note that social media is a fast-moving target and the directions I share for all social media sites were written in 2012; by the time you're reading this it is possible some of the specifics may have changed.

help you edit it. Read it aloud to yourself. If you were a high-powered professional, would you email back? Once the answer is yes, you know you have it right. Then, try submitting it to a few people you'd like to meet. Start with those you're mildly interested in so you can test your email and see if it works. If it does, start emailing the professionals higher on your list.

Though these emails may seem intimidating at first, I assure you they're simple to write. Why? Because they're all about you and your dreams. If I had to write these messages to accountants or IT professionals, I wouldn't know what to say, because those aren't the fields that interest me. However, if you love technology and your dream is to be an IT professional, writing emails to IT professionals will be easy and you'll naturally connect with someone in that field. All you have to do is be yourself, be sincere, and let that person know how much you admire them. If you do that, you can't go wrong.

Of course, making the request is only the first step. Now you have to set up the meeting and make the most of those 15 minutes. This chapter is only as valuable as the ones that follow, so I'll see you on the next page.

Note: before you start emailing professionals, you must make sure you have a professional email address that features your first and last name and a professional signature. I explain how to do this at

isaadney.com/freestuff

Chapter 18

The Art of Setting an Appointment

LINDA

> *"Reach out when you need help and don't be afraid. Others are willing to help because they know life isn't easy. And when someone is willing to help you, a whole new world of possibilities seems to instantly appear."*
>
> —Miami Dade College & Georgetown University

IF YOU'VE READ the previous chapters carefully and followed the directions exactly, you're now getting responses from professionals who are willing to talk with you for 15 minutes. This is the most crucial time—when you must turn an email connection into an in-person connection.

You need to make the informational interview appointment.

Don't panic—this is easy, but if done wrong, it can mess up everything you've accomplished thus far to make a connection with this person. The correct approach takes mature, professional communication skills, but once you get into this habit it will seem effortless.

When you hear back from the professional that he'd love to meet with you, send an email that looks something like this:

Hi *[insert name here]*,

Thank you so much for getting back to me! It means more to me than you know.

I am so excited to learn from you and cannot wait to meet with you for 15 minutes to ask a few questions about your current job, what it takes to be successful, and any advice you might have for me.

I know you must be busy, so I truly appreciate you meeting with me. Currently, I am free next Tuesday 9/18 between 8 a.m. and 1 p.m. and Friday 9/21 from 11 a.m. to 3 p.m. Please let me know if any of those times work for you and where would be most convenient for us to meet (I am happy to stop by your office).

If none of the above times work, please let me know what will be better for you.

Thank you again *[insert name here]*. I am so excited to meet you.

Sincerely,

Your Full Name

Student *[if you hold an office in a club you can mention that here, such as student, SGA Vice President]*

Name of Your College

Email *[your email must be professional—I recommend your first and last name]*

Cell Phone *[this is especially important when setting up the appointment, as you'll want to have each other's phone numbers in case something comes up last minute or in case you get lost.]*

By now, you're probably noticing the patterns in these emails. The key in this one is to give two choices of days and times (choose two days about a week after the date of the e-mail as your contact will probably already be booked that present week) for the person to meet with you. Then he can glance at his calendar and email you back with the time you can meet and the location.

Usually it's most convenient to meet professionals where they work, but sometimes they suggest a coffee shop, which can be nice. If they do that, always offer to buy the coffee. If they offer to buy for you first, politely refuse once, but if they insist, go ahead.

If you're trying to set a phone interview with someone who doesn't live in your area, use the same email template, but instead of asking where to meet, request a phone number and the best time to call.

Any connection you make through email, social networking, or on the phone can be valuable, but nothing replaces in-person meetings. Always do everything you can to have those— especially once you figure out exactly what you want to do.

Once the professional emails you back with a time and place, respond back briefly to say thank you and that you look forward to meeting him *(something like: Thanks so much [insert professional's name here]. I look forward to meeting you at [insert time and place here]).* If you aren't sure how to get to the office, check the company website and an online map first. If you're still unsure, feel free to ask in the email response, but be sure to show initiative here, and don't act helpless. Always take the phone number with you so you can call ahead if you're delayed by traffic or get lost. (Of course you'll give yourself extra time to get there). If you don't have his number, add "My cell is 555-555-5555. What's the best number to reach you on the day of the appointment in case I get lost? Thanks again!"

These templates will help get you started and show you the general principles behind professional communication. In short, be courteous, be brief, be yourself, and make it incredibly easy for the professional to make an appointment with you.

Chapter 19

How to Talk to Strangers–
Making the Most of the Informational Interview

DAVID

"*I spend a lot of time talking with people who work in careers I find interesting. They provide valuable insight into what classes I should take and what opportunities I should look for.*"

—College of the Sequoias in Visalia & University of California at Merced

SO NOW ALL YOU have to do is show up—right? If you're like most students, meeting a stranger for the first time can seem as intimidating and awkward as a blind date, but do not fear. It doesn't have to be that way. If you use what I teach you in this section, meeting strangers for the first time will become easy and incredibly fun.

When preparing for your meeting, the first thing to do is make sure you have a professional outfit to wear[10] and a nice portfolio or notepad to bring your questions and take notes with (bring your updated resume[11] as well, but do not give it to a professional unless asked). The easiest part about an informational interview is that you're there to learn, which means you don't have to do much talking. The key is to listen

---

10   To read the article I wrote for *USA Today College* on dressing professionally go to www. isaadney.com/freestuff

11   I think you know what I'm going to say here—go to your career center to create your resume!

and to ask strategic questions that allow the professional to do most of the talking and reveal valuable information and advice.

When you arrive, shake the professional's hand, thank him again for meeting with you, express your understanding that he's incredibly busy, and, that as stated in the email, you only intend to take 15 minutes of his time. Then re-state why you're interested in learning from him and ask your first question.

He may ask a bit more about you first, so feel free to answer, but don't spend much time talking about yourself. Highlight key points that differentiate you (your college, major, background, and why you're interested in this particular field/industry).

Now you're ready to ask the best questions to elicit the most information you can get in 15 minutes. Be sure to make note of the time and don't stay beyond your limit. If the professional insists you can go on longer, feel free—but let him insist first. Assume all you have is 15 minutes, and be sure to respect the professional's time (if the interview goes well, you can always follow up to have another meeting). Since you don't have long, you'll want to make the most of the time to make a genuine connection and learn as much as possible. There are many ways you can do this, but I found the five questions below are the best ways to discover if the professional's job is a good fit for you and learn insider secrets for success. These questions fit nicely into the 15-minute time frame:

1. What was your college experience like, and how did it lead to where you are today?
2. What do you love most about your job?
3. What is the most challenging part of your job?
4. What are the most important skills and qualities someone needs to be successful in your job?
5. What advice do you have for someone like me who would love to do a job like yours one day?

As you progress in doing informational interviews and become more comfortable with exactly what you want to do, you'll develop your own questions and tailor each interview to help you gain the knowledge you need, but when in doubt, these five questions always work and will give you incredible knowledge about that professional and his profession. Sometimes, I would bring extra questions in case the person answered quickly and we had more time. I also found the more questions I took with me, the less nervous I felt. The best questions are specific to the job and open ended, allowing your contact to tell you a story or share advice. Don't ask anything personal, especially regarding salary and benefits. The goal is to learn about his career path and what he thinks is important for success in that particular industry. If you walk out of an informational interview learning those two things, you'll know you've done it right.

While these formulas may seem daunting, I only share them with you to alleviate the pressure. Infuse your own style and personality into these meetings, and most importantly—just be yourself. The rest will fall into place and you'll find yourself with life-changing connections and amazing opportunities.

Chapter 20

The End is Only the Beginning

ALEX

> *"Always maintain communication with people who helped you become the person you are today. They are pivotal to your success, and will continue to be. Keep them informed, and always let them know how appreciative you are. Strengthening that bond will make the biggest difference in both your personal and career development."*
> —Seminole State College of Florida & University of Central Florida

NOW YOU KNOW everything you need for your first successful informational interview. I could go on and on about the incredible benefits of this process, but the only way you'll truly know is by following through. Do not wait! Start now. You'll find this is much easier than you think.

The best part is: once you've finished the informational interview, your relationship with that professional isn't over. In fact, it has only begun. If you meet someone and discover her job or the industry she works in isn't for you, you still need to follow up because she has excellent advice and guidance to share when it comes to the professional world. And for those you meet who do exactly what you want to do, proper follow-up is even more important and valuable.

To turn informational interviews into long-term mentoring relationships, internship opportunities, and jobs, follow up is key. Below are the steps to take to make the most out of the informational interview after it happens:

- Say thank you with a note or email immediately after the interview. Thank your contact person for her time and mention a piece of advice or information that truly resonated.

- About a week later, take a piece of advice the person gave you. This might be connecting with another person, visiting a particular website, applying for a particular internship, or reading a book. Then follow up by letting her know you took her advice and explaining how it helped you.

- If you clicked with a particular professional and you're interested in his or her job, ask if you could job-shadow her for a day to get a closer look at what the position entails.

- About once a month (or any other appropriate intervals depending on how close you've become with this person) send brief updates on any success you've had related to the advice/guidance she shared with you.

- Whenever you have another related industry or professional question, send him or her a quick email for follow-up advice.

- If you ever have an interview for an internship or a job in that industry, email the professional asking for her advice. You can ask her to look over your resume and cover letter and/or give you interview tips.

- And finally, once you feel you've built a comfortable and genuine relationship with the professional, ask if she has any advice regarding how to get an internship at her company or in her industry. If you're about to graduate, feel free to ask the same advice about full-time jobs. The key is to wait and ask this after you've built a relationship.

Conclusion

While it may seem like a lot of work to locate and connect with professionals to learn what you want to do with your life and find an internship and a job, if you engage in this process naturally and sincerely, you will have access to the hidden job market and save yourself from a possible lifetime of misery in a job you hate. Ask anyone who doesn't enjoy his job and he'll tell you that investing in yourself early to figure out what you want to do is worth it. A small investment of time and energy now will help you discover a path that excites you *and* provide the connections to get you there.

In many cases, the professionals you meet with will be so impressed by your eagerness and desire to learn that they'll offer internships and other opportunities on the spot. However, you cannot count on this, and that isn't the most important reason to meet with them. As always, the value of these professional mentors in your life will take you far beyond getting an internship or job. They will give you guidance. They will give you support. They will give you advice that—if you take it—will change your life. Because often, all it takes is one shift in perspective, one person who believes in you, and one opportunity.

The rest is up to you.

The Only Guaranteed Investment

By this time, I hope you've figured out community college success is about much more than showing up for class and getting good grades. It is about people. It is about hard work; it is an investment in *yourself.*

Investing in your success during this crucial time in life is one of the only guaranteed investments you can make.

I'm talking about putting everything you have—your creativity and all the resources and people around you right now—into your education, job search, and future. This kind of belief in yourself takes time, energy, and hard work. The good news (and one of the best parts about community college) is that it doesn't take that much money. Sure, tuition may seem like a large sum when you're working to pay the bills, but this is pennies compared to the money you can make later.[12] The great jobs go to students who have the courage to do more than just go to class and go home. These students have the persistence to visit their professors during the first week of class, and the maturity to step outside their comfort zones to make connections and get ahead. If you *act* on everything you've learned in this book, you will go far in life.

If you take anything from this book, I hope you realize *you are worthy of greatness* and *you are the only person standing in your way.* Until you truly accept and believe you have the power to change the course of your own life, nothing will happen. If you harness your amazing strengths and talents and ask others for help, you will succeed. Henry Ford said "whether you think you can or you think you can't, you're right!"

This is a turning point in your life. Let it be the moment you say, *"I can succeed."* Don't hesitate to reach for your goals. Don't be afraid to sacrifice. Don't be afraid to fail or to start from the bottom. Don't hold back from whatever it takes, and don't hesitate to enjoy this journey and rise above average— even when it seems everyone around you is settling for less. Never settle. Believe you're a worthy investment, and then buy up all the stock.

If it takes a while for you to believe in yourself, just remember this: *I believe in you.* I know you're someone I can believe in because you're reading this book. Writing this book took hard work and sacrifice, and *you* are the only thing that got me through it. I imagined you turning the pages and finally knowing you can do more with your life. I imagined you finally believing you're the best investment in the world. I imagined you deciding to believe in yourself and do whatever it takes to climb higher, try harder, reach the top, and help countless people in your community do the same.

---

12 Go to www. isaadney.com/freestuff to learn more about how to work less and work smarter so you'll have time to invest in yourself and pay your college tuition.

This book exists because of you. And from the bottom of my heart, I thank you for investing in your community college success. Your achievements will create a huge ripple effect for your family, your community, and our world. When you reach higher, you challenge everyone around you to do the same.

Community college is an incredible opportunity to learn, grow, and connect with people who will change your life for the better. This is your time to embark on a journey of purpose, hope, and success beyond your wildest dreams. Community college is your opportunity, right here, right now, to transform your life. Only you can make the most of that opportunity. And the good news is:

You are not alone.

Student Stories

I HOPE YOU ENJOY reading the following stories of struggle and triumph, as well as words of advice from community college students like you—my friends from my online community of college success at facebook.com/ccsuccess. I hope you join us if you haven't already.

These students have won more than 70 prestigious awards and over $750,000 in scholarships. They are incredibly successful student leaders. However, many of them started like me, and maybe you too—scared and alone, wondering where this new step would lead. Once they connected with others and diligently pursued that college degree, they achieved success beyond their wildest dreams. Below they share their stories and their secrets so you can learn from their experiences, win scholarships, and have great success. I think you'll find a lot of yourself in these stories.

Obstacles

How students struggled and overcame obstacles to get their college educations.

Failing Out of College the First Time

ASHLEY

"I was my own worst obstacle. I went to college right out of high school when I wasn't in the right state of mind or at the right maturity level. I dropped all my classes and had to pay a lot of money back. After working really hard I learned having a degree does make all the difference."

—Pasco-Hernando Community College

MELISSA

"When I started college, I was ill-prepared for being in the "real world" as I had led a very sheltered life. I transferred to a four-year college far away from my parents, trying to figure out how I could be me. I quickly failed out of my dream college, because I was too busy living life to attend class. A few years ago I decided to give it another try, this time selecting a community college. I enjoyed the smaller class sizes and the fact that my professors cared about me, plus I could take classes online."

—Front Range Community College

STEVE

"When I went to college for the first time at Ohio State, I was a first-generation college student from a background of limited financial means who never graduated from high school. In approximately one year I went from being homeless to being enrolled in college, but I didn't have the support of parents, high school counselors, or even friends to guide me through the college application, admissions, and orientation process. I felt completely lost.

"I stayed at my Ohio State orientation only long enough to get my ID; I thought I was finished. I ordered all my books online because it was cheaper, but they were several editions too old, though at the time I didn't understand why that mattered. Ultimately, I never saw an advisor, I enrolled in classes I didn't need, I was poorly equipped for those classes, and I didn't do well.

"Fortunately, I realized this and decided to cut my losses until I was more ready. I moved to Florida, where I was able to learn enough to enroll in community college by speaking with my new college-educated friends. My wonderful community college provided resources to assist me during my entire journey. Furthermore, being in the workforce for several years at a company that demanded excellence helped me develop the kind of focus and dedication to make my second college experience more successful."

—Valencia College & Emory University

Fearful of Starting College

SANA

"I was scared I wasn't going to go anywhere after attending a community college, but that idea changed when I met so many influential people who went to community colleges."
—Seminole State College of Florida

CYNTHIA

"Making the decision to go to college was difficult. I was on my own, so I had to figure out how to balance school and life. This turned out to be the best decision of my LIFE, and thanks to scholarship foundations I am able to dream big."
—Bronx Community College & New York University

GRACE

"As a dual-enrolled, home-schooled student, I felt terrified of being in a classroom. I wasn't sure I'd like my professors, get along with my classmates, or get good grades. I decided to attend my first day of class with all the enthusiasm I could scrounge up and forget my fear. By doing this, I was able to see I did like my professors and classmates, and I'd be able to get good grades too."
—Seminole State College of Florida

KRISTINA

"My first day in college was one of the worst experiences I've ever had. I felt lost and alone. I didn't know what to do. I don't know how I overcame my fears, but all I remember is that I started school with tears in my eyes."
—Seminole State College of Florida

MATTHEW

"Upon returning to school, my number one fear—battling my disabilities—came to fruition. However, I decided I was going to take a proactive stance in my life, take charge, and make things happen."
—Massasoit Community College

MICHELLE

"I was scared I wouldn't measure up and would be the person lurking in the back of the class because I was older, wouldn't fit in, or wasn't smart enough. I related my high school experience to community college, but the two experiences couldn't have been more different. Once I realized that was the case, I became comfortable and just went for it!"

—Quinnipiac University

AUSTYN

"At first I really didn't want to attend college, and I started off at a 1.3 GPA. I did a lot of soul searching and finally decided getting a college education was the right thing to do."

—Seminole State College of Florida &
University of Central Florida

ANEAL

"I had to run away from home to pursue my college education against my parents' will. I moved from Toronto, Canada to Boca Raton, Florida. The greatest thing that helped me overcome obstacles was being determined and staying true to myself."

—Palm Beach State College

Lack of Finances to Afford College

NAHIRIS

"Lack of financial resources and being a refugee with limited English made college a difficult obstacle. However, through perseverance, hard work, and the fortune of being awarded Phi Theta Kappa and Jack Kent Cooke Foundation scholarships, I was able to continue my education."

—College of DuPage &
Boston University School of Medicine

DAVID

"My biggest obstacle to getting my college education was trying to find the funding. The Internet was an excellent source for finding different ways to pay for school."

-College of the Sequoias in Visalia &
University of California at Merced

ALEJANDRA

"*As an international student, I was scared about not being able to graduate due to financial barriers. I overcame my fear because I knew being scared wouldn't solve my problems. Fear would stagnate my plan for getting an education, so I needed to get rid of it.*"

—Palm Beach State College &
University of Miami

DAVID

"*I was scared about leaving my full-time job to become a full-time student. As a non-traditional student, I don't have parents to help me and I was worried about money. I overcame my fears by thoroughly researching funding before returning to college.*"

—College of the Sequoias in Visalia &
University of California at Merced

ERICA

"*Financial need has always been an obstacle to my college education. However, I joined programs and took leadership positions that gave me scholarships, and I received grants from the federal government. I also worked many jobs to save money for books, tuition, and living expenses, while still maintaining excellent grades and finding plenty of time to be involved in extra-curricular activities. You can't let your finances get in the way of your success.*"

—Seminole State College of Florida &
Florida State University

Stories of Non-Traditional/Adult Students

HEATHER

"*I had a few obstacles in going to college. I was a teen mother at the age of 16 and lived on my own, working two jobs to survive with little help from others. Later, after twenty years of struggling, I returned to school to pursue a degree. This lesson has taught me that you're never too old to learn.*"

—Mesa Community College &
Northern Arizona University

CHRISTOPHER

"For me, it seems obstacles have played a big role in my learning abilities. Diagnosed with ADD while in my twenties, and with a form of dyslexia, I found it tough to accomplish anything. When I first attended college in 2001, I wasn't committed to it and trying to work through my learning disabilities made things even more difficult. I dropped out or failed most of my classes and became discouraged. Maybe school wasn't for me. Maybe I wasn't meant to get a degree. These questions, and more, filled my thought process for many years following my failed first attempt. Fast-forward ten years later — after many different jobs along the way, something was always in the back of my mind saying, go back … try again. So, in the summer of 2011, I returned to school.

"Now 30 years old, I was ready to take on the monster again. I learned how to deal with my issues through counseling and how to use them to my benefit. Currently, having just finished my second term, I received A's in all six of my classes and currently have a 3.7 GPA (could be a 4.0 but had to transfer classes from ten years prior).

"While I believe college is a great place to find out WHAT you want to do with your life, it has served a different purpose for me. College helped me find out WHO I am. It helped me see more of who I am and brought to light obstacles I needed to conquer. Not until I knew who I was could figure out what I wanted to do or accomplish in college.

"I had the opportunity to attend a leadership retreat at Seminole State and that retreat helped me learn more about my personal and leadership qualities and how they would help me succeed. If you have the opportunity to attend a leadership retreat or conference at your college, please do so. It will help you connect with your peers and better prepare you for your future—both in school and afterward."

—Seminole State College of Florida

JEREMY

"When I started college at age 26, I was scared I wouldn't be able to handle the course load or keep up with the rest of the class. I made a commitment to not miss class and always turn in my assignments on time. I didn't realize how fast I would catch on to things."

—Pikes Peak Community College &
Colorado State University (Pueblo)

HEATHER

"I was nervous to come back to school after twenty years. Seeing so many younger students was nerve racking. I felt out of place and quite embarrassed, honestly. But I didn't let it get to me, and I actually was able to use my life skills to help other people."

—Mesa Community College &
Northern Arizona University

First-Generation Students and Those Who Felt Alone

GARY

"As the first person in my family to attend college, it was challenging for me because my family had no idea what I was going through, and I couldn't rely on them to help me through it."

—Jefferson College & University of Tampa

LINDSEY

"Being a first-generation college student is scary. It can hinder your success, but only if you let it. I didn't grow up in a family where my parents had the knowledge or experience to prepare me for college."

—St. Johns River State College

KRISTIN

"I did not have the support of my parents to help with my college application process because they weren't with me. I was all alone."

—Seminole State College of Florida

JOSHUA

"I never got help from my family, so I worked hard and studied hard to make my grades."

—Pensacola State College

VANESSA

"I faced many fears when attending college, especially being the first in the family to pursue a college degree. It was hard not having anyone in my family who'd gone through the whole experience, and I wondered if I would be able to advance, pass my classes, and graduate. I also constantly wondered why I was going to college, what my purpose was, and if I was making the right decisions. It was a long process to overcome these doubts, but eventually I learned I can make a difference and do something with my life. Now I can show my family how."

—Seminole State College of Florida &
University of Central Florida

SUNIL

"I had the obstacle of coming to a new country and being on my own. This was hard because I didn't understand the system, but I told myself I would be successful at the highest level, regardless of the circumstances."

—Broward College

Advice

Top secrets and advice from students who've won over $750,000 in scholarships and achieved great success in their lives.

Push Yourself Beyond Your Comfort Zone

GARY

"Push yourself. I never let myself get comfortable with where I was. I was on the All-USA Today academic team, a Scholar Laureate, and Student Leader in Missouri. There's no way that I could have achieved any of this if I was comfortable. Keep pushing."

—Jefferson College & University of Tampa

LINDSEY

"Broaden your horizons. Work at a summer camp in your field of study. Volunteer. Put yourself out there, despite the discomfort. Talk about what you're doing every chance you get. You never know what contacts or opportunities you might run into."

—St. Johns River State College

CHRISTOPHER

"You can always handle more than you think. Know your limits, but push them."

—Rochester Institute of Technology

STEVE

"I attribute my success in being the Valedictorian and Distinguished Graduated of my community college as well as winning a Phi Theta Kappa award and the Jack Kent Cooke Undergraduate Transfer Scholarship to fortune, good ideas, and the passion to see it all through. My advice to any community college students who want to make themselves successful is to try. While the advice to "try" seems a bit cliché and simplistic, I think it's the advice most needed by community college students.

"If you never put yourself out there, apply for that scholarship, run for that position, take that harder class with the well-connected professor, then you can't possibly be successful.

"Too many students at community college seem convinced of their inevitable failure and intrinsic inferiority before they even attempt an action; they need to let that go. In all truth, the only thing that separated me from many of my peers was my willingness to step up and take a risk. I cannot overemphasize the importance of that. Also, get involved. The number of opportunities you'll encounter and the dedication to service you can demonstrate by being involved will help distinguish you from others for any potential future schools, employers, and scholarships."

—Valencia College & Emory University

ANGELICA

"Don't be afraid to set ambitious goals. It's up to you to decide your future. With determination, action, and curiosity, many things can be achieved and these goals become more real as you explore them. Don't ever stop moving forward! You know your own pace."

—Seminole State College of Florida &
Stetson University

ERICA

"Sometimes college scares me. I'm afraid I won't be able to afford the tuition, and I'm afraid I won't do well in my classes. The thing is, I refuse to ever sink to the level of my fears. I always rise above them and realize I can do anything and everything I want in life, and I can be great. At times I may have to work two jobs and will have to study hard for every class, but I know I can do it. And I will do it."

—Seminole State College of Florida &
Florida State University

STEVE

"Take risks. There's always an excuse NOT to do something. I too had car payments, a job to worry about, and rent to pay. I too was worried about my loans and finding scholarships and how I would go to school and pay my bills. Talk to your friends, your family, and your employers. Figure out what your options are and make calculated decisions about how best to get where you want to go.

"Decide whether success in college is valuable to you or not, and if it is, then start making other life decisions based around that fact. I took out around $13,000 in loans to help pay for my first two years in school so I could scale back my work and still survive. That sounds like a lot of money, but I don't regret that decision in the least. It gave me the freedom to work hard enough to get into a good school and earn scholarships that are taking care of the rest. Thirteen thousand dollars for a $200,000 education is a small price to pay."

—Valencia College & Emory University

SABRINA

"When I first started in community college, I was okay with being average. I got good grades but never went above and beyond. Then I realized I shouldn't be afraid to succeed or fail, because if you never take a chance you'll never know what wonderful things might happen. Success builds your confidence and mistakes help you learn. Either way, whatever decisions you make or don't make, YOU are the only person at the end of the day who has to live with your decisions."

—Seminole State College of Florida &
University of Central Florida

MIKHAIL

"Set optimum standards of success and never deviate from them. Do not be too hard on yourself, and learn more from your failures than you do from your successes."

—Valencia College & the University of Tampa

ERICA

"Use all the resources available to you. First of all, you're paying for them through tuition and fees. Secondly, it will take you from average into greatness. Everything your college has to offer will benefit you. Get involved in programs, visit the career centers often, and attend events for networking. Use your time wisely, because you won't be able to re-do any semesters."

—Seminole State College of Florida &
Florida State University

Focus on Grades

DAVID

"Getting good grades is the name of the game. Treat this as a full-time job. If you get good grades, you win the best scholarships. Winning scholarships makes top universities affordable. Those grades will make you the best at your profession."

—College of the Sequoias in Visalia &
University of California at Merced

Stay Organized

ALEJANDRA

"Time management is crucial. It is possible to do it all! Developing proper study habits is important as well, because figuring this out can save you a lot of time. Discovering what type of learner you are and studying accordingly not only allows you to save time, it also gives you the best results."

—Palm Beach State College &
University of Miami

SHIENA MARIE

"Planning and organization are the keys to everything. Use an organizer to write down all your classes and anything you have to do. Don't wait untill the last minute to get your paper work for transferring. Always plan ahead and make numerous back-up plans."

—Northwest Florida State College

Enlist Help from Other People

SHIENA MARIE

"Communication is vital at a community college. Apply for as many scholarships as possible, even if you don't think you can win or qualify. You never know until you try. Always do your best and play to win."

—Northwest Florida State College

STEVE

"Don't be afraid to sell yourself to others. You have strengths: figure out what they are and how to demonstrate them to others. Doors will open for you without a lot of personal effort if others view you as competent and dedicated to a cause. Don't be afraid to let other people know you have skills, or that you're exceptionally good at something. Talent isn't something to be ashamed of, and other people don't have a magical ability to recognize your strengths if you don't share them."

—Valencia College & Emory University

LINDA

"I attribute my success to the faith and inspiration from my mentors, the support I received from family and friends, and the hard work and determination to not only transform myself, but more importantly, to transform the lives of others."

—Miami Dade College &
Georgetown University

Stay Focused on Your Goals and Never Give Up

KRISTINA

"My ability to constantly move forward in life, no matter what, and my decision to set aside my fears are the main characteristics that helped me win so many awards in college. My advice to other students is to ignore everyone who tries to discourage you, and be confident you can succeed."

—Seminole State College of Florida

SUNIL

"The first step to being successful is conditioning your mind, so no matter what challenges arise, you will overcome them. Once you have that mindset then you just need to pursue your goals. Get involved in your schoolwork and the opportunities that arise."

—Broward College

MICHELLE

"I attribute my success, such as winning the Jack Kent Cooke scholarship, the Quinnipiac University Merit Transfer Scholarship, the Student Leader of the Year Award, and many more to being focused. I used to tell everyone I was a linebacker coming through because no one could take my eyes off the goal. I focused on each immediate goal until it was completed. If you focus on school in that manner, then you'll do well. Once you let distractions play a part in your success, and take your eyes off the prize, then you'll pay the price in grades, in interest, and in the way you start to think about school."

—Quinnipiac University

NAHIRIS

"Never, ever give up. Follow your passion and don't let bumps on the road take you away from your goals. Find a good mentor and listen to advice. Surround yourself with positive and passionate people. Be respectful and polite."

-College of DuPage &
Boston University School of Medicine

MIKHAIL

"I attribute my success to my driven personality and the fact that I learned to choose my battles when it comes to understanding and accentuating my strengths, rather than accepting any and every challenge presented."

—Valencia College & The University of Tampa

SUNIL

"The road to success is not straight: it is narrow, curvy and is full of bumps. But if you ride out the storm, good weather will come!"

—Broward College

MATTHEW

"I've struggled with learning disabilities and ADD. Through hard work, perseverance, and strong mentors at my community college I've been able to strive for excellence."

—Massasoit Community College

JEREMY

"Have a clear list of priorities and goals in writing and review them often. Read or listen to a book about time management. Develop a mental picture of where you want to be in five or ten years and start acting the part."

—Pikes Peak Community College &
Colorado State University (Pueblo)

MIKHAIL

"I was scared about underachieving and failure when it came to attending college. I overcame these fears by realizing fear is paralysis and I am only human."

—Valencia College & the University of Tampa

ALEJANDRA

"I attribute my academic and scholarship success to the support and love of my family and friends, as well as my own perseverance. I advise you to always keep your goal in mind. Staying focused is one of the most important things you can do when facing challenges. If you know what you want the outcome to be, then you know the adversities are not there to stay; they only reinforce how badly you want your dream to come true."

—Palm Beach State College &
University of Miami

Recommended Resources

I'd like to say a special thanks to all the incredible authors and organizations who endorsed *Community College Success*. I only approached people I admire and whose work I love. Below is information about their incredible work, plus many more books and websites that changed my life.

BOOKS

NOTE: I highly recommend all these books, but since I realize not everyone is an avid reader (though you should work toward it), I starred the top five books I consider *must-reads*.

Getting Better Grades
How to Win at College by Cal Newport
How to Become a Straight-A Student by Cal Newport

Procrastination
Eat That Frog by Brian Tracy

Communication with Professors
Say This NOT That to Your Professor by Ellen Bremen

Finding Money for College
The College Solution: A Guide for Everyone Looking for the Right School at the Right Price and *Shrinking the Cost of College* by Lynn O'Shaughnessy www.thecollegesolution.com

College Life - General
The Everything College Survival Book by Susan Fitzgerald
Living College Life in the Front Row by Jon Vroman
The Naked Roommate by Harlan Cohen

My Favorite Networking Books
How to Win Friends and Influence People by Dale Carnegie
The Little Black Book of Networking by Jeffrey Gitomer

Motivation
DRIVE by Daniel H. Pink

Finding a Job and Managing the 20-Something Crisis
They Don't Teach Corporate in College: A Twenty-Something's Guide to the Business World by Alexandra Levit

20 Something, 20 Everything, and *The 20 Something Manifesto* by Christine Hassler

Earn What You're Really Worth by Brian Tracy

What Color is Your Parachute by Richard Nelson Bolles

Guerrilla Marketing for Job Hunters 3.0: How to Stand Out from the Crowd and Tap Into the Hidden Job Market using Social Media and 999 other Tactics Today by Jay Conrad Levinson and David E. Perry

On Student Success
The Five Factors Theory by Dr. Angela Long

Recommended Student Success Course Curriculum
The Hero's Journey—An Introspective and Critical Thinking Approach to Life/Career Planning by Dr. Pat Ferguson

Your Life as a River: Reflecting on the Past to Build a Strengths Based Future by Dr. Therese Lask

Becoming a Master Student by Dave Ellis

Inspiration

Living Proof by Lucas Boyce

Chicken Soup for the College Soul by James Malinchak, Jack Canfield, Mark Victor Hansen, Kimberly Kirberger, and Dan Clark

How to Be Like Walt and *Read Your Life: 11 Ways to Better Yourself Through Books* by Pat Williams

The Other Wes Moore by Wes Moore

My Favorite Fiction Authors

I've included these because so many people ask. Fiction is a wonderful way to invigorate your mind and improve your writing and vocabulary:

Jeannette Walls

Marisa De Los Santos

Kristin Harmel

Sophie Kinsella

Carolyn Parkhurst

Kathryn Stockett

Douglas Kennedy

Self-Help

*7 Habits of Highly Effective People by Steven Covey

The Happiness Project by Gretchen Rubin

Self Matters: Creating Your Life from the Inside Out by Phillip C. McGraw

SUCCESS Magazine www.successmagazine.com

RESOURCES

My Favorite College Blogs

The Chatty Professor www.chattyprof.blogspot.com

Cal Newport's Blog www.studyhacks.com

(Because I love fashion) www.collegefashion.net

For English Language Learners
Easy English News—a monthly newspaper for English language learners elizabethclaire.com/store/easy-english-news.html

Innovative Educational Organizations
Financial Literacy Programs for College Students at Financial EducatorsCouncil.org

Free Online Mentoring at StudentMentor.org

Phi Theta Kappa Honors Society for two-year students www.ptk.org

National Council on Student Development (NCSD) www.ncsdonline.org

The League for Innovation in the Community College www.league.org

National Institute for Staff and Organizational Development (NISOD) www.nisod.org

Motivational College Speakers
Adam LoDolce www.ultimatesocialfreedom.com

Jon Vroman www.frontrowoncampus.com

Joshua Fredenburg www.visionxy.com

James Malinchak www.malinchak.com

My Favorite College News Sources (where I go to get the scoop)
The New York Times www.thechoice.blogs.nytimes.com

Lumina Foundation News www.luminafoundation.org/tag/lumina_news

The Chronicle of Higher Education www.chronicle.com

The Wall Street Journal www.online.wsj.com/public/page/news-career-education-college.html

Campus Overload www.washingtonpost.com/blogs/campus-overload

USA TODAY College www.usatodayeducate.com/staging

Community College Times www.communitycollegetimes. com

Community College Spotlight www.communitycollegespot-light.org

Keeping informed about world news is important for networking, conversation starters, and improving your ability to contribute to the world. Talk to your school about college readership programs with the nation's best newspapers, such as the *New York Times* and *USA Today*.

Contact Isa

isa@communitycollegesuccess.com

Join the Community and Share Your Story
Facebook.com/ccsuccess
Twitter.com/isaadney
YouTube.com/isaadney
Blog: communitycollegesuccess.com

Hear Isa Speak
Would you like to meet Isa? Do you think the message in this book would change the lives of students at your college or at your next event? Learn more about her motivational speaking at www.isaadney.com/speaking or email info@isaadney.com to check availability.

Use Community College Success in the Classroom or in a Book Club
For activities and discussion questions that help make *Community College Success* an excellent supplemental resource for a College Success course, First Year Experience course, First-Generation Program, or a book club, visit www.isaadney.com/freestuff.

Free Books for Students

We would love to make free copies of *Community College Success* available to students who will benefit from the tips, strategies, and advice to help them complete college and achieve success in their lives. Students who can't afford to buy this book are the ones who need it most.

If you're part of a company that's interested in corporate social responsibility—especially in the area of education—or you'd like to donate books to a local college, please contact us for further information:

NorlightsPress.com
762 State Road 458
Bedford, IN 47421

Telephone: 888-558-4354
Email: publisher@norlightspress.com
On the Internet: www.norlightspress.com

Acknowledgements

I DON'T HAVE ENOUGH pages in this book to adequately thank everyone who played a part in helping me get to where I am today—including making my dream come true to publish this book.

I want to thank my agent Krista Goering for believing in me and my book from day one. Thanks to Sammie, Dee, and Nadene at NorLightsPress for embracing my book with such enthusiasm. And a special thanks to Cal Newport for responding to an email from a first-time author. Without you, Cal, I would never have found Krista.

I thank my parents Robyn and Tomas Rosado for loving me and encouraging me every day of my life. The world would be a better place if everyone had parents like you. Also thanks to my extended family members who taught me so much about hard work, sacrifice, and the kinds of things money can never buy. I thank my brothers Tito and Robby for all the silly and joyous things we did together while growing up. You helped me develop the creativity to write this book, and I am so proud of you guys.

Thanks to my husband, partner, and best friend Jeremy for supporting me in this dream and dreaming along with me, and to the Adney family for laughing and crying with me throughout this journey.

I thank the Seminole State College of Florida faculty and staff for providing me with the incredible community college and professional experiences that inspired this book. I also thank the faculty and staff at Stetson University—especially Dr. Watts,

Dr. McFarland, Andy Dehnart, and Rosalie Carpenter—for making my transfer experience more than I could have ever imagined.

I'm grateful to the Jack Kent Cooke Foundation for all the work they do to make the Jack Kent Cooke undergraduate transfer scholarship a reality. This scholarship has been more than a life-altering financial opportunity for me—the community created by each staff member and scholar changed my life and gave me the courage to dream big and write this book. You taught me that people can move mountains when someone expects them to be great. Thanks to my fellow scholars who inspire me daily. I'm honored to count you among my best friends.

Thanks to MyLien, Miguel, Lori, Ale, Linda, Tatiana, Mikhail, Steve, Dan, Mark, and Tiffany for the conversations that taught me it's always more fun to think big and dream big with friends.

I appreciate all the friends I made at Seminole State College of Florida, especially those in Phi Theta Kappa and the Art and Phyllis Grindle Honors Institute. Thank you for showing me how powerful having friends in community college can be, and how beautiful it feels to have the kind of friends who cry out of happiness for your successes.

I thank all my faithful blog readers, Twitter followers, and Facebook friends: you bring me daily joy. And thank you to all the students who shared their stories in this book.

I'm grateful for each professional mentor who has answered my emails, shared fifteen minutes in a phone call or in your office, and bestowed wisdom upon me. Your kindness and graciousness inspired this book as you reminded me good people in this world are willing to share their knowledge if only someone asks. I can trace every professional success I've had to one of you and I can never fully show you my appreciation. This book is one way I hope to pay it forward.

I thank every student I met as a Student Life Coordinator at Seminole State College of Florida, especially those in the Florida College System Student Government Association, Phi Theta Kappa, The Honors Program, The Hope CommUnity

Center, Seminole State Volunteers, the Leadership Challenge Team, and the Student Engagement Team. This book would not exist without the passion, fire, dedication, drive, intelligence, and leadership you showed me every day.

And finally, this book is dedicated to you and every community college student I will meet in the future. You inspire me more than you will ever know.

About the Author

ISA GRADUATED FROM Seminole Community College (now called Seminole State College of Florida) where she received a $110,000 Jack Kent Cooke Scholarship. She transferred to Stetson University where she graduated at the top of her class and received her B.A. in Communications. She will finish her M.Ed in Training and Development from the University of Illinois at Urbana-Champaign in June 2012 and currently works as a Student Life Coordinator at Seminole State College.

Her blog, communitycollegesuccess.com, has been featured in *USA Today, Community College Spotlight, The Network Journal, The National Society of Collegiate Scholars, BrainTrack. com* and *LA Weekly.* She is a motivational speaker at colleges across the country and conducts workshops on networking, diversity, and leadership.

Isa has spoken for organizations such as the National Council on Student Development (an affiliate council of the American Association of Community Colleges), Phi Theta Kappa, The Hope CommUnity Center (an advocacy and support center for migrant farmworkers and their families), Pasco-Hernando Community College, Gulf Coast State College, The Florida College System Student Government Association, and one of the Nation's largest universities, The University of Central Florida.

Adney is married and lives in Orlando, Florida.

To learn more about Isa, visit

www.isaadney.com

Additional Endorsements for Community College Success

"Isa Adney has tapped into the heart and soul of the true community college experience. Her words of wisdom will ring true for students who are willing to find the inspiration, motivation, life direction, and human connections needed for higher education achievement. Community colleges offer a grounded, exciting, and honorable first-year experience for those privileged enough to choose it. As a proud community college graduate myself, I cannot agree more with her treasured advice to reach beyond oneself and initiate positive relationships. I thank God for the foundational beginnings that were given to me at a community college and wholeheartedly recommend this book as it is written to engage, unlock, and speak to the heart of every potential student leader!"   –Dr. Angela Long,
national speaker and author of the *Five Factors Theory*

"Isa Adney is helping break the negative stigma associated with students who go to a community college. I know from firsthand experience that the tips Isa provides in this book are guaranteed to help any student on the path to professional and educational success. This book is a resource, and success starts with getting involved and using your resources. Any student who wants to better themselves needs to read this book ASAP."   –Shiena Marie E. Normand,
student at Northwest Florida State College

"As president of my Phi Theta Kappa chapter at my community college, a first generation college student, and owner of Leadership Messenger Academy, I was able to pull real, effective strategies from this book to promote my business and myself as a student. Isa offers tools and resources I have never found in any other book about school or business, and I will read and re-read this book and suggest it to everyone I know. If you're beginning your college career and have any doubts about how well you will do as a student, this is the ONE book you need."   –Gary Dees, student at
Jefferson College and University of Tampa

"Community college students are empowered to take control of their futures through the incredible wisdom offered in this book. I just wish this book was available when I was in college, because I know how transformative it will be for college students."
–Ashkon Jafari, Co-Founder of StudentMentor.org

"*Community College Success* is a must-read book for high school students, returning students, and/or first-generation students searching for tips to successfully navigate their educational journey at a community college. By chronicling strategies and lessons learned through her own story, Isa Adney provides resources and practical advice for rising above average. This groundbreaking book is written by a community college graduate specifically for community college students – mentoring them on how to succeed and complete their educational goals."   –Coral Noonan-Terry, Interim Director, National Institute for Staff, and Organizational Development (NISOD)

"For the more than 12 million students enrolled in community colleges across the United States, Isa Adney's *Community College Success* will serve as a valuable and vital guide to the community college experience. From how and why to shoot for the stars, to the importance of forming relationships with peers and mentors, to how to use community college as a stepping stone to your future, Isa – herself an award-winning community college alumna – will lead readers through everything they need to know to excel. An invaluable tool from an author who will, by the time you finish reading, feel like your mentor and friend!"   –Kristin Harmel, author of seven novels including *The Sweetness of Forgetting*

"Community college students now have a passionate ambassador and dynamic spokesperson: Isa Adney. Isa's own community college success and her encouraging, do-able advice is an inspirational and important motivator for every two-year college student who feels 'less than' for choosing this path."   –Ellen Bremen, author of *Say This NOT That to Your Professor* award-winning community college professor (NISOD, NCIA, Sloan Consortium)

"Isa Adney's story is as special as it is relevant for young people looking for an opportunity for higher education. Her story not only inspires – it educates and empowers as well. The tools Isa shares in her book are invaluable to anyone looking for an opportunity to build upon skills in networking, community involvement, and leadership. It's also a must read for academic authorities seeking to make a difference in the life of the students they serve."   –Lucas Boyce, author of *Living Proof*

"Community College Success provides an incredibly helpful roadmap for students who want to not only succeed in college, but also make valuable connections for their ultimate careers."
–Lynn O'Shaughnessy, author of
The College Solution and *Shrinking the Cost of College*

"This book will change your life. It is a guide. It will inspire you. Isa's book clearly outlines simple yet effective strategies for tapping into valuable resources that will set you apart from the crowd and propel you forward to the next level of community college success."
–Jon Vroman, author of
Living College Life In The Front Row and
Founder of Front Row Foundation.

"Community College Success gives students valuable insight that can help them rise above average and maximize their higher-education experience. With the current economic situation, budget cuts are impacting our students support services. Ms. Adney provides clear and caring guidance our students need to help effectively navigate the community college system."
–Vince Shorb, Chief Marketing Officer,
National Financial Educators Council www.
FinancialEducatorsCouncil.org

"The college world is a new, foreign country for many students who are the first in their families to go to college. I know it was for me. A book such as *Community College Success*, had it been available way back then, would have made a big difference. It should be recommended reading for college freshmen and their families."
–Elizabeth Claire, Editor of "Easy English NEWS"

"A.A. degrees are now referred to as the new Master's degree in many circles, given the large number of professionals who are going back to community colleges to obtain the affordable, useful work skills employers are demanding today. In this terrific work, Ms. Adney has provided a practical step-by-step guide for helping people navigate this unfamiliar world – and maximize every penny of their educational investment."   –Matt Youngquist,
Founder of Career Horizons

"Isa Adney's book is an amazing resource for the future success of our nation because it provides emerging leaders within community colleges with specific strategies that will help them attain education, leadership, and career success in the 21st Century."
        –Joshua Fredenburg, National Speaker, Leadership Expert, President and Founder of Circle of Change Leadership Conference

"Here's an opportunity to learn from a book written specifically for community college students, providing important lessons on how to succeed."   –Dr. Therese Lask, author of *Your Life as a River: Reflecting on the Past to Build a Strengths Based Future*

"Community College Success is a phenomenal snapshot of the community college landscape. A must read for all students, faculty and staff."   –Dr. Pat Ferguson, author of *The Hero's Journey – An Introspective and Critical Thinking Approach to Life/Career Planning*

Available from NorlightsPress and
fine booksellers everywhere

Toll free: 888-558-4354   **Online:** www.norlightspress.com
Shipping Info: Add $2.95 - first item and $1.00 for each additional item

Name _____

Address _____

Daytime Phone _____

E-mail _____

No. Copies	Title	Price (each)	Total Cost

		Subtotal	
		Shipping	
		Total	

Payment by (circle one):
   Check   Visa   Mastercard   Discover   Am Express

Card number_____3 digit code_____

Exp.date_____ Signature_____

Mailing Address:
762 State Road 458
Bedford, IN 47421

Sign up to receive our catalogue at
www.norlightspress.com